CITYSPOTS
COLOGNE

Jo Whittingham

KU-579-800

Written by Jo Whittingham
Updated by Kate Hairsine

Published by Thomas Cook Publishing
A division of Thomas Cook Tour Operations Limited
Company registration No: 1450464 England
The Thomas Cook Business Park, 9 Coningsby Road
Peterborough PE3 8SB, United Kingdom
Email: sales@thomascook.com, Tel: +44 (0)1733 416477
www.thomascookpublishing.com

Produced by The Content Works Ltd
Aston Court, Kingsmead Business Park, Frederick Place
High Wycombe, Bucks HP11 1LA
www.thecontentworks.com

Series design based on an original concept by Studio 183 Limited

ISBN: 978-1-84157-870-5

First edition © 2006 Thomas Cook Publishing
This second edition © 2008 Thomas Cook Publishing
Text © Thomas Cook Publishing
Maps © Thomas Cook Publishing/PCGraphics (UK) Limited
Transport map © Communicarta Limited

Series Editor: Kelly Anne Pipes
Production/DTP: Steven Collins

Printed and bound in Spain by GraphyCems

Cover photography (Martinsviertel) © Ray Juno/Corbis

CONTENTS

SYMBOLS KEY

The following symbols are used throughout this book:

ⓐ address **ⓣ** telephone **ⓦ** website address
ⓛ opening times **ⓝ** public transport connections

The following symbols are used on the maps:

ⓘ	information office	▪	points of interest
✈	airport	○	city
✚	hospital	○	large town
⛊	police station	○	small town
🚍	bus station	═	motorway
🚆	railway station	—	main road
Ⓤ	U-Bahn	—	minor road
Ⓢ	S-Bahn	—	railway
✝	cathedral		
❶	numbers denote featured cafés & restaurants		

Hotels and restaurants are graded by approximate price as follows:
£ budget price **££** mid-range price **£££** expensive

Abbreviations used in addresses:
Str., -str.   Strasse, -strasse (street, road)
Pl., -pl.   Platz, -platz (square)

◑ *Morning view of Cologne town houses*

Introduction

As well as having Germany's most-visited tourist attraction –
the imposing cathedral, the biggest Gothic building in the world –
Cologne is a thriving metropolis with world-class art galleries,
fabulous shopping, cosy Christmas markets, a fun-loving population,
good beer and a vibrant alternative scene. But despite being an
excellent city-break destination, Cologne is a surprisingly well-kept
travel secret.

With a population of just over a million, Cologne is Germany's
fourth largest city, and the economic and cultural capital of the
Rhineland region. Its inhabitants have a reputation for being laid-
back and tolerant, one of the reasons why Cologne has a large gay
community and is a magnet for many artists and musicians.

The city's history stretches back more than 2,000 years to its Roman
founders and plenty of evidence of their influence can still be found
on the streets and in museums. More recent history can be felt in
the old town's cobbled alleyways, the majority of which were rebuilt,
along with the churches, after devastating World War II bombing.
The surviving historic architecture is set against mostly attractive
modern neighbours.

Art and culture are in plentiful supply in Cologne. Its galleries are
full of important international works and superb collections by famous
local artists. This, combined with the huge selection of theatres,
concert halls and music venues, makes it difficult for even the most
dedicated cultural tourist to do more than scratch the surface of
the city's cultural riches in a short break.

Cologne is one of Germany's leading gastronomic centres, boasting
more than 3,000 restaurants and pubs, and food from almost all
corners of the globe can be enjoyed here, alongside hearty traditional

German fare. Cologne's café culture seems almost Mediterranean during the summer, when the streets are filled with people relaxing over coffee, lunch or enormous ice creams. But it's at night that the city really comes to life, with local *Kölsch* beer consumed enthusiastically in traditional pubs, and cocktails prepared at trendy bars and clubs every night of the week.

The friendly people of Cologne save their best for the annual festivals, however, when they, along with hundreds of thousands of visitors, throng the streets for the colourful *Rosenmontag* (Rose Monday) and Christopher Street Day parades, as well as the awe-inspiring *Kölner Lichter* (Cologne Lights) firework display.

● *The cathedral is visible from kilometres away*

When to go

SEASONS & CLIMATE

During the summer, life moves outdoors and everyone drinks and dines at tables under huge parasols in the streets and squares, come rain or shine. There are usually spells when summer temperatures reach about 30°C (86°F), but the norm is a more comfortable 18–25°C (65–77°F).

Winter rarely brings heavy snow to the city although there can be cold snaps. It is best to expect mild and wet weather from winter into spring, but in a vibrant city like Cologne a little rain needn't get in the way of a good time (see pages 46–7).

ANNUAL EVENTS

Cologne regards itself as a festival city and rightly so, because it hosts events that attract millions of visitors throughout the year, some of which are steeped in tradition and the rest just involve having a good time. During the festivals you will see the city at its busiest and most colourful, but remember to book your room well in advance.

February

Karneval (31 Jan–6 Feb 2008, 19–24 Feb 2009) Carnival in Cologne is one of Europe's biggest street festivals and a good excuse to don fancy dress and party from the Thursday before Ash Wednesday through to **Rosenmontag** (Rose Monday) without sobering up. But be warned, if you aren't into massive drunken crowds and 24 hours a day of oompah music reverberating around every corner of the city, then carnival isn't for you (for more about *Karneval*, see pages 12–13). Ⓦ www.koelnerkarneval.de

● *Christopher Street Day is one of Europe's biggest Gay Pride events*

April

Art Cologne Germany's most important art fair is attended by more than 250 international galleries and dealers, showing the best modern and contemporary works the world has to offer. Open to the public as well as to trade, this six-day fair is packed full of exhibits, performances and events. Organisers moved the traditional date from November to April in 2008, so check the website for details. Ⓦ www.artcologne.de

July

Christopher Street Day More than just a day, this Gay Pride gathering has taken over the first weekend in July, when there is an open-air stage in the old town and the city's most vivacious parade, as up to 35,000 lavishly costumed lesbians and gays party through the streets and on late into the night. Ⓦ www.csd-cologne.de

Kölner Lichter (Cologne Lights) (12 July 2008, 11 July 2009) A spectacular firework display above the Rhine, set to music and watched by hundreds of thousands of revellers from the river's banks and bridges. Arrive early to bag a good spot. Ⓦ www.koelner-lichter.de

Summerjam Germany's largest reggae festival, this three-day event is held in July every year on Cologne's Fühlinger Lake, less than half an hour out of the city on public transport. Ⓦ www.summerjam.de

July–August

SOMA – Summer of Music and Arts Festival Held on the banks of the Rhine, this three-day festival is an insider tip for chilling out and hearing great alternative music at open-air stages and in club tents. There's a great kids' area and free camping Ⓦ www.soma-festival.de

November–December

Christmas markets From the last weekend in Nov to Dec 23, six markets fill Cologne with festive spirit. Ideal for finding traditional German Christmas decorations, toys, nutcrackers and treats, they are a great antidote to the stresses of modern Christmas shopping. The huge market in Roncalliplatz is watched over by a gigantic Christmas tree and the immense cathedral. This, and the other city centre markets in Alter Markt, Neumarkt and Rudolfplatz, are free to visit; the floating market moored at Rheinpromenade and the Medieval Market next to the Chocolate Museum charge admission.

Ⓦ www.koeln.de/en/whatson/christmas/markets

PUBLIC HOLIDAYS
New Year's Day 1 Jan
Good Friday 21 March 2008, 10 Apr 2009
Easter Monday 24 March 2008, 12 Apr 2009
Labour Day 1 May
Ascension Day 1 May 2008, 21 May 2009
Whit Monday 12 May 2008, 1 June 2009
Corpus Christi 22 May 2008, 11 June 2009
German Unification Day 3 Oct
All Saints' Day 1 Nov
Christmas 25 and 26 Dec

There is some regional variation in German public holidays, but the dates above are correct for Cologne. Most shops and businesses in the city close in the afternoon of: *Weiberfastnacht* (the Thursday before Rose Monday), Rose Monday, Christmas Eve and New Year's Eve, as well as the whole day on the public holidays shown above.

Karneval

A GUIDE TO CELEBRATING CARNIVAL IN COLOGNE

Karneval (carnival) in Cologne is considered to be the 'fifth season' and kicks off on 11 November at 11.11 sharp at the Heumarkt square in the old town, followed by a day of fancy dress and drinking. But it's the six days before the start of Lent on Ash Wednesday that mark Cologne's real party season. On *Weiberfastnacht* (Women's Carnival) on the Thursday before Ash Wednesday, thousands of costumed merrymakers, mainly women, gather at Heumarkt for the official opening of celebrations by the Carnival Prince, Peasant and Maiden at exactly 11.11. Be warned – on this day women traditionally run around with scissors and cut off men's ties as trophies, giving them a kiss as recompense.

On the Friday and Saturday, the party frenzy continues in Cologne's pubs and spills out into the street. It you don't want to stand out as a tourist, don't forget to bring a costume with you (most supermarkets and stores sell face paint and masks during carnival, so there's no excuse not to enter into the carnival spirit).

Joining in the alternative *Geisterzug*, or Ghost parade, is a fun option on Saturday night. Unlike the Rose Monday procession, anyone can parade in the *Geisterzug*, which every year weaves and dances its way through a different part of the city, accompanied by hundreds of drummers. For more information on the route, ask at the tourist office or take a look at Ⓦ www.geisterzug.de (in German).

On Carnival Sunday at 11.00 is the time when Cologne's children and district clubs parade in costume through the city's streets. It's smaller than the Rose Monday procession, but takes virtually the same route.

Rosenmontag (Rose Monday) is the highlight of Cologne's carnival, when the kilometre-long parade twists through town. More than a million people line the streets to cheer on the decorated floats and scramble for sweets and flowers. Many of the carnival groups spend the whole year preparing their floats, often topped with huge figures satirising topical events. The tourist office publishes a free map of the parade route, and you need to get up early to secure a good viewing spot.

The fifth season wraps up with the burning of the *Nubbel* (the spirit of carnival) to atone for the sins of the past five days. Many pubs and restaurants will torch a straw figure at midnight on Tuesday, before the city returns to normal on Ash Wednesday.

Large parts of Cologne are closed to traffic on Carnival Sunday and Rose Monday, and it is an exercise in futility to attempt to drive anywhere in the city centre on those days. Allow plenty of time if you are planning on taking the tram or underground: the public transport system virtually grinds to a halt during carnival. And if you plan on sleeping at some stage in the five days, don't forget to bring earplugs – in many parts of the city, carnival music blares incessantly during the fifth season. And don't forget to say, 'Kölle Alaaf' – 'Cologne above all'.

🔺 *Dressing up for Rosenmontag*

History

It was the Romans who realised that this spot on the Rhine would be a good place to settle, and in 33 BC Colonia was born. Thanks to the fact that a local girl later married the Emperor Claudius, it was elevated to city status by 50 AD. As well as their engineering expertise and military might, the Romans also later brought Christianity to the city, which went on to become a centre of ecclesiastical importance over the centuries.

The emblem of the city's prosperity and power, the huge cathedral (the Dom) was to be the 'largest structure north of the Alps' when it was started in 1248. It was the archbishops of Cologne who wielded much of this power, not only within the church, but also in secular matters. However, by the 15th century the citizens had driven the archbishops out and Cologne was one of the wealthiest German-speaking cities, but the gigantic cathedral construction project would not be completed for another 600 years (see page 61).

◐ *The giant Dom, 600 years in the making*

In 1794, the city was occupied by French soldiers, who chose to renumber the houses according to their own system. They happened to mark the house of the Muelhens family 4711, and the name of their famous brand of eau de cologne was born. This concoction had been made in the city since the early 18th century and was originally sold as medicinal water, but in 1810 Napoleon decreed that the formulas of medicines should be made known for the benefit of the poor, so to retain their secret the manufacturers reneged on their medicinal claims and reclassified it as a toilet water. The scent was popular with bath-shy aristocrats, who used it to mask their own unpleasant odour.

Cologne and the Rhineland were annexed in 1815 by the kings of Prussia, under whose rule the city continued to prosper, becoming a hub of the new railways in the mid-19th century and finally completing its cathedral in 1880. This success as an industrial and communications centre continued into the 20th century, only to be abruptly halted by World War II.

Hitler's army occupied the previously demilitarised Rhineland in 1936, but in early 1940 troops gathered in Cologne to launch an invasion of the Netherlands, Belgium and France. This prompted the first Allied bombing raid on the city and subsequent raids on military and industrial targets intensified until the last, most devastating attack on 2 March 1945. Cologne was reduced to a pile of rubble, with as many as 90 per cent of its buildings and all of its bridges destroyed, although the cathedral survived.

Immediately after the war the resilient population began the reconstruction of their city and managed to restore something of the historical character to the old town area, painstakingly rebuilding and repairing the ancient Romanesque churches. Despite its turbulent past at the heart of Europe, Cologne has again grown into a prosperous media and industrial centre, and a beautiful city.

Lifestyle

Germans think of Cologne as a fun-loving city and local *Kölsch* people are renowned for their openness, laid-back attitude and sharp sense of humour. A cynic might say that such stereotypes are manufactured by tourist officials to draw in the crowds, but in Cologne such claims seem to have considerably more than a grain of truth. The patient locals do their best to help tourists who can't speak German and are not easily offended. In fact if you adopt the local habit of sitting in busy cafés or beer gardens, you'll find it easy to get chatting with the locals, who will be happy to give their tips for good bars, clubs and places to visit. People of all ages spend a lot of their time socialising on terraces in front of cafés and restaurants in summer and in cosy bars in winter. Although alcoholic drinks are available day and late into the night, the atmosphere in bars and on the streets remains friendly rather than intimidating.

Cologne is an important centre for Germany's media and arts, and it has a large university and music colleges, all of which may account for the bohemian lifestyle that many of its inhabitants seem to enjoy, hanging out in cafés and bars until late and frequenting theatres and galleries. Spending sunny Sundays in the park picnicking and working on their tan is another popular pastime, and it is normal to see bikini-clad women on any patch of grass.

Germany has recycling its rubbish down to a fine art and Cologne's litter bins have separate sections for paper, plastic and general waste, so take care that your rubbish goes in the right place and whatever you do don't drop litter – nobody else does.

● *Cologne café society – laid-back and sociable*

The only downside is that Cologne is not a particularly cheap place to stay, shop or eat. The demand for hotel rooms is high during the festivals and the many trade fairs and conferences held in the city, so prices are inflated over these periods. Although visitors from the UK might still find Germany a little cheaper than home, for those from the US it will seem expensive.

Culture

For outsiders, the perception of Cologne as an industrial city sits comfortably with the assumption that it has little culture to offer. Nothing could be further from the truth, because the city's long history provides ample material for museums and its wealthy art collectors have left a world-class legacy for its galleries.

In just two of the old town galleries – Museum Ludwig and the Wallraf-Richartz Museum – spectacular art collections cover everything from medieval triptychs to still lifes by Dutch masters, Impressionist landscapes to pop art, right up to contemporary German pieces. All of this can be found inside the box-like buildings of these two museums (see pages 64–7), which, despite their severe appearance, provide beautiful, sensitive and well-lit gallery space inside. Unsurpassed bodies of work by well-known local artists Käthe Kollwitz (see page 80) and Max Ernst (located in Brühl, see page 138) fill entire galleries of their own that have both recently opened, providing incredible insight into their fascinating lives and works of art. There are other art venues spread around Cologne, devoted to ecclesiastical, Asian and applied art, that are all worth visiting if time allows. Most galleries and museums are closed on Mondays but open on public holidays (with the exception of Christmas and New Year's Day) when opening hours are the same as for Sundays.

Those interested in Roman artefacts will be captivated by the relics of old Colonia on display in the main Römisch-Germanisches Museum (see pages 66–7), including the famous Dionysus mosaic, but should not miss a walk through a Roman sewer and the foundations of the Roman governor's palace in the Praetorium under the town hall (see page 66).

After suitable quiet contemplation of art and history, this energetic population likes to be entertained. All kinds of theatre,

⬤ *The Philharmonie is just one of Cologne's many cultural venues*

usually performed in German, from traditional regional humour to experimental new German and international productions, and huge international musicals and stage shows, can be found in venues of all sizes around the city. The quality of classical music in Cologne is extremely high and the city is home to a number of music schools. Performances by the Gürzenich-Orchestra Cologne, which can trace its origins back to the 15th century, and the WDR Symphony Orchestra Cologne, with its great reputation for performing the work of 20th-century composers, are always in demand. These are the two resident orchestras at the *Kölner Philharmonie* (Philharmonic Hall) (see page 64), where performances are given almost daily. Popular classical concerts are also given in the city's 12 Romanesque churches, which provide a wonderful atmosphere in which to enjoy the work of famous composers. While perhaps not renowned for opera, Cologne does have an excellent Opera House, which hosts a varied repertoire of modern and classical operas, along with frequent ballet performances.

Many of Cologne's cultural highlights are in or near the centre of the city, so even on a short visit you will be able to sample a few. Theatre and concert listings and tickets can be obtained at individual venues or from Köln Ticket (☎ 0221-2801 🖅 www.koelnticket.de).

Another option is to buy a Cologne Welcome Card, which gives discounts to many museums, theatres and other venues, as well as free travel on the combined public transport network. Available from the tourist office (see page 152).

Remember, all of Cologne's museums are closed on Mondays (except if the Monday happens to be a public holiday).

▶ *A glass of* Kölsch *is a great early-evening pick-me-up*

Shopping

Germany has deregulated its shopping hours, so while many stores and supermarkets in Cologne close at 20.00 Monday to Saturday, some of the bigger chains are in the process of extending their hours. Most shops in Germany are closed on Sundays, although Cologne has a multitude of small kiosks where it's possible to buy everything from beer to bread rolls seven days a week.

The city has a maze of shopping streets reserved just for pedestrians and once you get started it will be a while before you want to find your way out. International and German designer names are well represented, as are stores packed with cheap up-to-the-minute fashion and brightly lit shops loaded with top cosmetic brands. Head to the city-centre streets of Hohe Strasse and Schildergasse, just a few minutes walk from the cathedral, for the big names, and wind your way out towards the ring road to find the trendy clothes and shoe stores on Ehrenstrasse, and individually designed jewellery on Friesenstrasse.

Goods are generally just slightly cheaper than they are in UK shops, a notable example being the luxurious German-made Dr Hauschka cosmetics, which are more widely available and reasonably priced here. Another fashionable souvenir is a pair of Birkenstock sandals from the brand's own shop on Breite Strasse.

Fortunately the regular souvenir shops are almost entirely confined to the cathedral square, so if you want to take home a model of the cathedral, some pretty hand-made Christmas decorations or a magnificent nutcracker you will find your quarry here. There is also a little *Kölsch* emporium on Alter Markt, selling everything related to the city's best-loved beer, including the slim, straight-sided glasses (*Stangen*) from which it is always consumed. Of course, by far the best souvenir from this city is a bottle of the scent that bears its name – *Kölnwasser* or eau de cologne. The best-known brand is 4711, so-called after the number of its inventor's house and packaged in pretty turquoise-labelled bottles. A reconstruction of that very building, on its original site at the corner of Glockengasse, is dedicated to the sale of the famous fragrance and though its fashionable days have long gone, taking a sniff here is an essential Cologne experience.

USEFUL SHOPPING PHRASES

What time do the shops open/close?
Um wieviel Uhr öffnen/schliessen die Geschäfte?
Oom veefeel oor erffnen/shleessen dee geshefter?

How much is this?
Wieviel kostet das?
Veefeel kostet das?

Can I try this on?
Kann ich das anprobieren?
Can ikh das anprobeeren?

My size is ...
Ich habe Grösse ...
Ikh haber grerser ...

I'll take this one, thank you
Ich nehme das, danke schön
Ikh neymer das, danker shern

Can you show me the one in the window/this one?
Zeigen Sie mir bitte das im Fenster/dieses da?
Tsyegen zee mere bitter dass im fenster/deezess dar?

This is too large/too small/too expensive
Es ist zu gross/zu klein/zu teuer
Es ist tsu gross/tsu kline/tsu toyer

Eating & drinking

In recent years Germans, like the British, have become more open-minded about their food and today Cologne is bursting with great places to eat. As a result of its ethnic diversity, the city boasts many fine Turkish, Italian and Japanese restaurants. British diners will note the scarcity of Indian restaurants, but the few around the centre serve excellent curries and anyone desperate for a spicy hit could try a *Currywurst* (sliced sausage in curry sauce) instead. Also, at the first sign of the sun, people of all ages will be out under parasols eating outrageously large sundaes in Italian ice cream parlours.

Many of the café/bistro-style places that line Cologne's streets open early enough to serve a German breakfast of bread, meat and cheese to locals and tourists, while the bakeries also open early for coffee and pastries. Both these options provide a cheap alternative to hotel buffets.

The city normally breaks for lunch between noon and 15.00, when anything from a sandwich or pasta dish in a café to a full-blown restaurant meal is tucked away. There are very few take-away sandwich shops, as people generally sit down to eat. Most cafés and bars, along with many restaurants, then stay open through the afternoon until late, perhaps 23.00 or midnight. Restaurants often double as bars and

PRICE CATEGORIES

The restaurant price guides used in the book indicate the approximate cost of a three-course meal for one person, excluding drinks.

£ under €20   ££ €20–30   £££ more than €30

diners will linger after dinner over a few drinks. Restaurant and bar closing hours are much more flexible than in Britain and the US, and places will often stay open later than their advertised hours if there is a crowd.

⬤ *Cologne's streets are lined with cafés and bistros*

LOCAL SPECIALITIES

Cologne's lifeblood is its *Kölsch*, a light and tasty top-fermented beer (where the yeast rises instead of sinking), brewed to a special recipe by numerous local breweries. Everyone, male and female, drinks *Kölsch* from special straight 0.2 litre glasses, known as *Stangen*. It is served almost everywhere, but for an authentic experience of *Kölsch* drinking go to a traditional brewery pub (*Brauhaus*) – a misnomer today, as no brewing goes on in them. The old town has many to choose from and they are distinguished by their dark wood-panelled interiors, plain sanded table tops and slightly over-confident waiters, who will swap your empty glass for a full one, sometimes without asking, until you tell them to stop. When you pay the bill, they will also more than likely rummage round for change in their black wallet until you tell them to keep it.

The *Brauhäuser* are also good places to sample local delicacies, but because of their popularity with locals and tourists alike, it is often a good idea to book a table, especially on weekends.

A long-standing Cologne joke, born out of story about a cheapskate host, is the dish *Halve Hahn*, which, although it means half a chicken, is actually a rye bread roll and cheese. A more serious meal is pork knuckle with pickled cabbage and mashed potato (*Haxe mit Sauerkraut und Kartoffelpüree*), definitely the dish of choice for meat-lovers.

Table service is universal in cafés and bars as well as restaurants, where generally service is not included and a tip of up to 10 per cent is normal, as long as you were satisfied with your meal. Beware that credit cards are not widely accepted, so it is advisable before you order to check that your card will pay the bill.

▶ Kölsch *isn't* Kölsch *unless it's served in a* Stange

In summer Cologne is perfect for a picnic and its many busy parks, particularly Rheinpark, Stadtgarten and Volksgarten, are inviting places for lunch. A respectable spread can be assembled from the bakeries and fruit stalls around Hohe Strasse, where you can pick up cakes, sandwiches and pretzels. For something more luxurious try the Kaufhof department store's basement supermarket, with its tempting deli counters and wine selection.

VEGETARIAN OPTIONS

Vegetarians travelling to Cologne might not be optimistic about their opportunities for fine dining given Germany's reputation as a nation of carnivores, but you will be pleasantly surprised. Although the menus in traditional restaurants and Brauhäuser are heavily meat-based, even in these places there are delicious cheese and mushroom dishes. The traditional garlic mushrooms with potato and salad (*Champignonköpfe gefüllt mit Kräuterknoblauchsauce*) are tastier and more substantial than they sound.

Another option is to try one of the city's diverse ethnic restaurants. Italian places will be the most familiar option, serving plenty of meat-free pasta and pizza, while most Thai, Chinese and Vietnamese restaurants have a small selection of vegetarian dishes. A safe bet is also to follow the students to the streets around Zülpicherplatz, where there are lots of falafel restaurants and all the cafés have vegetarian options. There are even some dedicated vegetarian restaurants around, one of the best and most stylish of which is near Friesenplatz:

Osho's Place £ Internationally inspired vegetarian food and salad bar in a relaxed, informal restaurant. ❸ Venloer Str. 5–7 ❶ 0221-800 0581 ❹ 08.00–24.00 Sun–Thur, until 01.00 Fri & Sat ❾ www.oshos-place.de

USEFUL DINING PHRASES

I would like a table for ... people
Ein Tisch für ... Personen, bitte
Ine teesh foor ... perzohnen, bitter

Waiter/waitress!
Herr Ober/Fräulein, bitte!
Hair ohber/froyline, bitter!

May I have the bill, please?
Die Rechnung, bitte?
Dee rekhnung, bitter?

Could I have it well-cooked/medium/rare please?
Ich möchte es bitte durch/halb durch/englisch gebraten?
Ikh merkhter es bitter doorkh/halb doorkh/eng-lish gebrarten?

I am a vegetarian. Does this contain meat?
Ich bin Vegetarier (Vegetarierin fem.). Enthält das hier Fleisch?
Ish bin veggetaareer (veggetaareerin). Enthelt dass heer flyshe?

Where is the toilet (restroom) please?
Wo sind die Toiletten, bitte?
Voo zeent dee toletten, bitter?

I would like a cup of/two cups of/another coffee/tea
Ich möchte eine Tasse/zwei Tassen/noch eine Tasse Kaffee/
Tee, bitte
*Ikh merkhter iner tasser/tsvy tassen/nokh iner tasser kafey/
tey, bitter*

I would like a beer/two beers, please
Ein Bier/Zwei Biere, bitte
Ine beer/tsvy beerer, bitter

Entertainment & nightlife

Cologne loves a good time. It is a youthful city, with a large student population, but people of all ages can be found enjoying a drink in one of the city's myriad bars, some of which stay open until 05.00. For those who fancy a dance, there are also plenty of trendy clubs to choose from, with DJs playing everything from rap and hip-hop to house and Latin beats.

As with most cities, different areas have their own style of bars and clubs and attract different crowds accordingly. The bars and traditional *Brauhäuser* in the old town are the standard tourist haunts, where *Kölsch* is consumed from lunchtime well into the early hours, particularly at the weekend. Meanwhile the locals hang out in the trendier bars and nightclubs on and around the ring road on any night of the week. Students congregate in bars and restaurants near Zülpicherplatz, and more fashionable types head north to the flash cocktail bars and expensive restaurants close to Friesenplatz.

Any norms are completely disrupted, however, when one of the city's festivals begins and the whole place gets party fever. This happens regularly and begins with the *Karneval* season on 11 November, which reaches its climax in February, with the Rose Monday parade, when the streets and bars are filled with two million revellers. July brings the Christopher Street Day parade, which is a huge Gay Pride event that draws almost as many visitors as *Karneval*, many of them in the most outlandish outfits imaginable. Later that month, the Cologne Lights, a fantastic firework display over the river, brings yet more crowds and provides another excuse to party. In between all this mayhem the city also has a vibrant live music scene, with its

stadium and arena hosting famous international pop acts and rock groups. Bands with smaller audiences also have plenty of venues to play in Cologne, and jazz is popular and easy to find in bars and the famous Stadtgarten venue in a city park. You can even hear excellent musicians, often students from local music schools, performing classical music around the cathedral square to help pay their fees.

After all this activity, sitting in a darkened room might appeal and a trip to one of many cinemas in town will cost you less than in the UK. Most blockbuster movies are dubbed into German, but several cinemas screen films in their original version with, or sometimes even without, subtitles. The website ⓦ www.choices.de gives an overview of all movies on in Cologne. It's in German, but scroll to the bottom of the page and click on 'Originalversionen' to see what's offered in English. The Metropolis Kino in Cologne's Südstadt (see page 118) specialises in English-language films and even has an English-language website and telephone line, making it easy to find out screening times.

Each venue has its own box office, but there are also conveniently located ticket shops in the city centre, which have comprehensive events listings and friendly staff to help you decide what to see.

KölnMusik Ticket ⓐ Roncallipl. (next to cathedral)
ⓣ 0221-2040 8160 ⓛ 10.00–19.00 Mon–Fri, until 16.00 Sat
KölnMusik Event ⓐ Mayersche Bookshop, Neumarkt
ⓣ 0221-2040 8333 ⓛ 09.00–20.00 Mon–Sat, until 21.00 Sat
Köln Ticket has an excellent listings website where you can also purchase tickets. It's in German, but is easy to work out.
ⓣ 0221-2801 ⓦ www.koelnticket.de

Sport & relaxation

SPECTATOR SPORTS

The RheinEnergie Stadium is home to the city's football heroes, FC Köln. Across the Rhine, in the Deutz district, the Kölner Haie (Cologne Sharks) play their ice hockey at Kölnarena. German league champions an amazing eight times, they have huge support in the city and the action-packed games make great entertainment.

While some may like to participate, most people probably prefer to watch the Ford Cologne Marathon, which starts from Mindenstrasse in Deutz late September/early October and sees 14,000 runners snake their way across the bridge and around the city. There is also an event for inline skaters, which you have to hope avoids the cobbles.

Kölner Haie/Cologne Sharks (ice hockey) ⓐ Kölnarena, Willy-Brand-Pl. 2, Deutz ⓣ 0221-8020 ⓦ Tickets and listings www.koelnticket.de or www.haie.de ⓝ U-Bahn: Deutz/Messe

FC Köln ⓐ RheinEnergie Stadion, Aachener Str. 999 ⓣ 0221-8021 ⓦ Tickets and listings www.koelnticket.de ⓝ Tram: RheinEnergie Stadion

🔺 *Cologne Sharks – the ice hockey team with bite*

Ford Cologne Marathon For route and entry information check the website. ⓦ www.koeln-marathon.de

PARTICIPATION & RELAXATION
Swimming
Outdoor pools are a summer favourite, but the **Eis- und Schwimmstadion**, close to the zoo, also has a climbing wall, basketball courts and a winter ice rink. The pool opens around the middle of May until the end of August. ⓐ Lentstrasse 30 ⓣ 0221-399 710 ⓛ 10.00–20.00 Mon–Fri; from 09.00 weekends and public holidays ⓤ U-Bahn: Zoo/Flora. Admission charge

Cycling
Cycling is popular with Cologne's residents and is a good way to see the city. If you hire a bike, stick to the clearly marked cycle lanes in town and the many large parks.
Radstation Köln Hbf is the place to hire bikes. ⓐ Breslauer Pl. (main railway station) ⓣ 0221-139 7190 ⓛ 05.30–22.30 Mon–Fri, 06.30–20.00 Sat, 08.00–20.00 Sun

Spas
Holidays are all about pampering, so treat yourself to a trip to a thermal spa where you can spend all day soaking in health-giving, mineral-rich waters and taking time out for a sauna, a massage or a beauty treatment.
Claudius Therme ⓐ Sachsenburgstr. 1 (Rheinpark) ⓣ 0221-981 440 ⓦ www.claudius-therme.de ⓛ 09.00–24.00 ⓤ Shuttle Bus 150 from Deutzer Bahnhof; U-Bahn: Zoo/Flora and cable car. Admission charge

Accommodation

This city relies on its trade fairs as much as tourism to fill its thousands of hotel rooms, so although there are many hotels to chose from they tend to cater to the needs and budget of the business customer rather than those travelling for pleasure. That said, if your visit to Cologne does not coincide with a trade fair or one of the major festivals you can pick up rooms quite cheaply, but if you descend with the hordes for a popular event, book as far in advance as possible and be prepared to pay a premium. In the city centre the only options apart from hotels are a few serviced apartments and backpacker hostels, which are also in demand during events.

Many tourists choose to base themselves in the *Altstadt* (old town) and this is sensible because it allows you to visit all the major sights on foot and means that there is only a short totter back to bed from the *Brauhäuser*. Therein lies one of the area's downfalls, however; it can be noisy well into the early hours of the morning, especially at the weekend, so if you don't plan to be out partying it would be wise to check your hotel's proximity to bars and nightclubs or find a room a little out of the centre. Staying away from the old town in Cologne's business or residential districts around the ring road, or across the river in Deutz, should be quieter and is certainly no less convenient

PRICE CATEGORIES

The ratings below indicate the approximate cost of a room for two people for one night.

£ up to €99   ££ €100–€199   £££ €200 and over

because the tram and U-Bahn system, along with the buses, will get you wherever you need to go cheaply and efficiently. Bear in mind that there are also numerous bars and nightclubs around the ring road between Rudolfplatz and Friesenplatz, so booming late-night bass could be an issue here too.

Cologne's star classification system for its hotels is voluntary, so while the ratings between 1 and 5 stars are good, if slightly generous, indicators of the facilities available, they are only displayed by some of the city's hotels, which is less than helpful.

The price categories box (unrelated to the official star system) gives an indication of the maximum rates that tourists in Cologne should expect to pay per night for a double room with a shower and toilet. The price is per room rather than per person. Breakfast is often included, but beware of expensive hotel breakfast buffets where it is not.

HOTELS

Am Rathaus £ Rather bare, but clean and functional rooms, right in the middle of the old town. ⓐ Bürgerstr. 6, 50667 ⓣ 0221-257 7624 ⓦ www.hotel-am-rathaus-koeln.de

Bremer £ Quiet, family-owned hotel close to the university, with good transport into the city centre. ⓐ Dürener Str. 225–227, 50931 Köln-Lindenthal ⓣ 0221-40 680 ⓦ www.hotelbremer.de

City Pension Storch £ Each of the simple, clean rooms in this small hotel comes with a kitchenette. Only five minutes walk to the Dom. ⓐ Steinfelder Gasse 26, 50670 ⓣ 0221-326 993 ⓦ www.city-pension-storch.de ⓝ U-Bahn: Appellhofplatz

Dom Hotel Am Römerbrunnen £ Budget accommodation with small rooms but friendly service right in the city centre. ⓐ Komoedienstr. 54, 50667 ⓣ 0221-16 094 ⓦ www.hotel-am-roemerbrunnen.com ⓝ U-Bahn: Appellhofplatz

Domgarten £ This pretty, old building has traditionally furnished rooms and a central location near the railway station. ⓐ Domstr. 26, 50668 ⓣ 0221-168 0080 ⓦ www.domgarten-hotel.de ⓝ U-Bahn: Dom/Hbf

Rhein-Hotel St Martin £ Right on the riverfront and at the centre of the old town, this is a good base from which to explore Cologne. ⓐ Frankenwerft 31–33, 50667 ⓣ 0221-257 7955 ⓦ www.koeln-altstadt.de/rheinhotel

Antik Hotel Bristol ££ Furnished with charming antiques, this reliable hotel is close to the MediaPark. ⓐ Kaiser-Wilhelm-Ring 48, 50672 ⓣ 0221-120 195 ⓦ www.antik-hotel-bristol.de ⓝ U-Bahn: Christophstrasse

Esplanade Hotel ££ Conveniently situated on the ring road, this friendly hotel has crisp, clean rooms and an excellent breakfast buffet. ⓐ Hohenstaufenring 56, 50674 ⓣ 0221-921 5570 ⓦ www.hotelesplanade.de ⓝ U-Bahn: Maritiuskirche

Hopper Hotel Et Cetera ££ This former monastery, located in the fashionable Belgian quarter, has stylishly furnished rooms. ⓐ Brüsseler Str. 26, 50674 ⓣ 0221-924 400 ⓦ www.hopper.de ⓝ U-Bahn: Rudolfplatz

Hotel Allegro ££ Well-priced hotel with excellent views of the Rhine River and excellent staff. ⓐ Thurnmarkt 1–7, 50676 ⓣ 0221-240 826 ⓦ www.hotel-allegro-koeln.de ⓝ U-Bahn: Heumarkt

🔺 *The Dom Hotel, comfort next to the cathedral*

Im Kupferkessel ££ On a quiet side-street off Christophstrasse, this friendly, family-run place has a traditional, beamed dining area and clean rooms. ⓐ Probsteigasse 6, 50670 ⓣ 0221-270 7960 ⓦ www.im-kupferkessel.de ⓝ U-Bahn: Christophstrasse

Crowne Plaza Cologne City Centre £££ Friendly service, comfortable rooms and a great location near Rudolfplatz make this a great choice. ⓐ Habsburgerring 9–13, 50674 ⓣ 0221-2280 ⓦ www.cologne-citycentre.crowneplaza.com ⓝ U-Bahn: Rudolfplatz

Dom Hotel £££ Completely refurbished in 2003, this excellent hotel, a member of the Le Meridien group, sits in the shadow of the cathedral. ⓐ Domkloster 2a, 50667 ⓣ 0221-20 240 ⓦ www.koeln.lemeridien.de ⓝ Train/Bus/U-Bahn: Dom/Hbf

Hotel im Wasserturm £££ This extraordinary hotel, with luxurious designer rooms, fills a 130-year-old water tower, close to the centre. ⓐ Kaygasse 2, 50676 ⓣ 0221-20 080 ⓦ www.hotel-im-wasserturm.de ⓝ U-Bahn: Poststrasse

SERVICED APARTMENTS

Domicilium £ Only 3 km (less than 2 miles) from the city centre, these stylish modern apartments are clean and comfortable. ⓐ Scheidtweiler Str. 15a, 50933 ⓣ 0221-546 3301 ⓦ www.domicilium-koeln.de ⓝ U-Bahn: Aachenerstrasse

Lyskirchen Altstadthotel £ Just south of the old town, eight well-appointed apartments are part of a standard hotel. ⓐ Filzengraben 26–32, 50676 ⓣ 0221-20 970 ⓦ www.hotel-lyskirchen.com ⓝ U-Bahn: Heumarkt

YOUTH & BACKPACKER HOSTELS

Jugendherberge Köln-Deutz £ This modern youth hostel has twin and group rooms with en-suite facilities. A Youth Hostel Association or Hostelling International membership card is required. ❸ Siegesstr. 5, 50679 ❶ 0221-814 711 Ⓦ www.koeln-deutz.jugendherberge.de Ⓝ Tram/Train: Köln Deutz

Station-Hostel for Backpackers £ Right next to the railway station, this basic but clean hostel has a great location, no curfew and some en-suite rooms. ❸ Marzellenstr. 44–56, 50668 ❶ 0221-912 5301 Ⓦ www.hostel-cologne.de Ⓝ Train/Bus/U-Bahn: Dom/Hbf

CAMPSITES

Camping Berger £ A well-equipped site with hot showers, shop and restaurant, situated on the bank of the Rhine about 7 km (4 miles) from the city centre. ❸ Uferstr. 73, 50996 Köln-Rodenkirchen ❶ 0221-935 5240 Ⓦ www.camping-berger-koeln.de Ⓝ U-Bahn: 16 to Rodenkirchen then Bus 135 to Uferstrasse

● *The Altstadt is a lively and convenient place to stay*

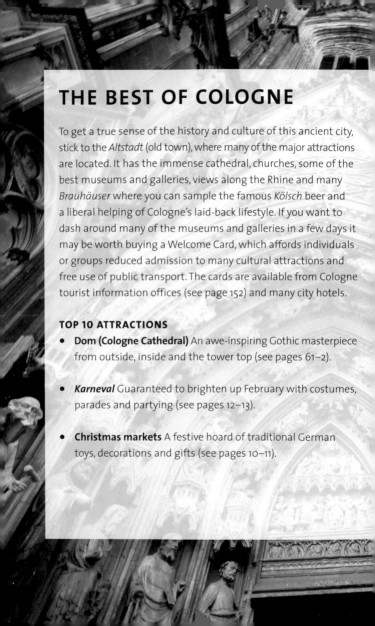

THE BEST OF COLOGNE

To get a true sense of the history and culture of this ancient city, stick to the *Altstadt* (old town), where many of the major attractions are located. It has the immense cathedral, churches, some of the best museums and galleries, views along the Rhine and many *Brauhäuser* where you can sample the famous *Kölsch* beer and a liberal helping of Cologne's laid-back lifestyle. If you want to dash around many of the museums and galleries in a few days it may be worth buying a Welcome Card, which affords individuals or groups reduced admission to many cultural attractions and free use of public transport. The cards are available from Cologne tourist information offices (see page 152) and many city hotels.

TOP 10 ATTRACTIONS

- **Dom (Cologne Cathedral)** An awe-inspiring Gothic masterpiece from outside, inside and the tower top (see pages 61–2).

- ***Karneval*** Guaranteed to brighten up February with costumes, parades and partying (see pages 12–13).

- **Christmas markets** A festive hoard of traditional German toys, decorations and gifts (see pages 10–11).

- **A tour of the Brauhäuser** (guided or otherwise) *Kölsch* drinking for research purposes (see page 70).

- **Museum Ludwig** A formidable collection of modern art in a beautiful interior (see pages 64–6).

- **Schokoladenmuseum (Chocolate Museum)** Learn about your favourite food and eat it (see pages 77–8).

- **Shopping** Everything from huge department stores to the quirkiest boutiques (see pages 22–3).

- **Römisch-Germanisches Museum (Roman Germanic Museum)** Packed with impressive and fragile artefacts (see pages 66–7).

- **Kölner Seilbahn (Cable car)** Probably the best view over the Rhine and the old town skyline (see page 111).

- **Thermal spa** Pamper yourself (see pages 33 and 104–5).

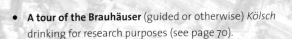
The exterior of the Dom, *Cologne's Cathedral*

Suggested itineraries

Your at-a-glance guide to seeing the best that Cologne has to offer, depending on how much time you have.

HALF-DAY: COLOGNE IN A HURRY

If a few hours are all you have, head to the Altstadt (old town). Stand outside the cathedral and marvel at its size, venture inside to see the exquisite gold Shrine of the Magi, then dash up the tower's 509 steps for a panoramic view of the city. Catch your breath over a *Kölsch* or ice cream in the cathedral square and choose to visit one of the Roncalliplatz museums: the Museum Ludwig for modern art or the Römisch-Germanisches Museum to discover Roman Cologne. Finally wind your way through the old town to a *Brauhaus* with a river view and enjoy a traditional meal.

1 DAY: TIME TO SEE A LITTLE MORE

As long as it isn't Sunday, add some shopping to the half-day highlights; in Hohe Strasse and Schildergasse if you are a chain-store devotee, or on Ehrenstrasse and Breite Strasse if boutiques are your style. There might just be time to squeeze in a trip to the chocolate museum and a few glasses of *Kölsch* in an old town bar.

2–3 DAYS: TIME TO SEE MUCH MORE

Once you have had your fill of the old town sights and the shops, pack a picnic, escape the city centre and get to Cologne zoo early for feeding time. When hunger gets the better of you take the cable car across the Rhine and find a spot with a view in the Rheinpark, where you can tuck in to lunch and relax. Spend more than you should on a slap-up meal on Friesenstrasse and sip cocktails in a trendy bar until late.

LONGER: ENJOYING COLOGNE TO THE FULL

If you have more than three days available, you have time to soak
up the atmosphere and embrace the café culture in the stylish areas
around the ring road at your leisure; explore the Belgian quarter and
stop for refreshments under the imposing medieval gate in Rudolfplatz.
For evening entertainment, experience some traditional Cologne
humour at Volkstheater Millowitsch or dress to impress and party
at one of the sleek clubs on Friesenplatz. There might also be time
to board a scenic cruise on the Rhine to see the city from a different
angle and some of the beautiful scenery that lines the river banks
outside Cologne. You should also take at least one trip out of town,
to Bonn or Brühl (see pages 120–40).

● *Make time to relax at the Botanischer Garten*

Something for nothing

If it's free entertainment that you are after, then Cologne is your ideal destination, because throughout the year the city hosts all kinds of events and festivals that bring thousands of people onto the streets to enjoy a friendly party atmosphere. The biggest day is *Rosenmontag*

⏷ *Cologne lit by the Cologne Lights*

(Rose Monday) in February, when the Carnival season reaches its climax and a gigantic procession of floats, bands and city-dwellers in fancy dress makes its way through the streets, with people throwing sweets and chocolate bars to spectators as they pass.

Christopher Street Day (Gay Pride) in July has become the summer carnival and brings the crowds out again for another colourful parade of fabulous costumes, music and dancers. The following weekend usually brings *Kölner Lichter* (Cologne Lights), a huge firework display over the river, played out in time to classic pop anthems, which sees the river banks, bridges and tour boats crammed with eager spectators. All of these events see the old town bars packed to capacity, so that revellers spill out onto the streets and keep the party going into the early hours of the morning.

Rather more sedate, but with a wonderful festive atmosphere, four of Cologne's Christmas markets, in the old town squares from the end of November through December, are free to look round, although you will most likely be tempted to buy the traditional decorations, toys, gingerbread and mulled wine.

Even when there is no festival on there is a great atmosphere in the old town, and a walk through its streets and along the river will take you past entertainers, historic sights and fabulous views. The city's many parks are also ideal for a stroll or even a picnic. Sunday is when the locals descend on their green spaces, so if you want to make up an extra player for a game of football or just want to see how locals relax, do the same.

One more freebie that might appeal: if you visit Phantasialand (see pages 135–6) on your birthday and you can prove your date of birth, you get in for nothing.

When it rains

Think of rain as an opportunity rather than a disaster, a chance to stop dashing between the sights and linger in the places that you like the most. This is a city where you can really immerse yourself in art, so spend a few hours contemplating the masterpieces of modern art in Museum Ludwig, or perhaps moving up the chronologically arranged floors of the Wallraf-Richartz Museum from the glowing gold of medieval works to the bold brush strokes of the Impressionists (see pages 64–7). There are few places where so many great collections of paintings are this close together, so take the opportunity to enjoy them.

Guaranteed to cheer up even the dullest day for adults and children, the Chocolate Museum (see pages 77–8) is full of interesting exhibits explaining the origins and manufacture of everyone's favourite pick-me-up, with a chocolate fountain that is as good as it sounds. Rain could also be the perfect excuse to spoil yourself with a day pass to the thermal spa (see pages 33 and 104–5), where you can bathe in naturally mineral-rich water or keep out the chill in a sauna.

Another way to stay dry is to explore Cologne's huge potential for shopping – all under one roof. The truly massive Galeria Kaufhof department store alone should keep even a half-hearted shopper busy for an hour or so, with a basement full of deli counters, chocolates, wines and little bars to stop for a drink and a snack, and floors full of fashion, cosmetics and shoes. There is also the Neumarkt Galerie shopping centre, with its distinctive upside down ice cream on the roof, which is full of all kinds of shops, cafés and restaurants in the dry (see pages 81 and 85).

For a cosy atmosphere on a miserable day, look no further than the old town's *Brauhäuser*, which will instantly warm you with their wood-panelled walls, free-flowing *Kölsch* and some of the heartiest, most comforting food in the world. If it's really horrible outside they might even have an open fire burning to make for an extra cosy experience. For listings of *Brauhaüser* in the old town, see pages 70–2.

◖ *Chocolate production at Cologne's Chocolate Museum*

On arrival

There is no need to worry about your arrival in Cologne. It is a safe city with an efficient, well-signposted public transport system and a friendly population that is usually happy to help visitors.

TIME DIFFERENCES
German clocks follow Central European Time (CET). During Daylight Saving Time (end Mar–end Oct), the clocks are put ahead one hour.

ARRIVING
By air
It is likely that you will arrive into the modern, glass terminal buildings at Köln/Bonn Airport, since this is the regional centre for low-cost airlines. This airport has excellent facilities and travel links to Cologne, which is only 15 km (9 miles) away. Both the arrivals and departures areas have plenty of restaurants and cafés, including 24-hour buffet bars. Bureaux de change and ATMs can only be found in the departures areas, however, so bring euros with you to avoid any inconvenience. If any problems arise there are information desks located in the departures area of Terminal 1 (between areas B and C) and Terminal 2 (area D), where you will find assistance.

It takes less than 20 minutes to reach Cologne city centre by rail. Trains are frequent and cheap, with a single fare to the city centre station (Dom/Hbf) on the S-Bahn costing €2.20. The airport's train station is situated downstairs between Terminals 1 and 2.

Shuttle busses nos. 670 or 161 run to the bus ranks behind the Dom/Hbf and cost the same as the train, but take 25 mins.

Taxis usually take 15 mins (depending on the traffic) but are by far the most expensive option, as the fare into the city is €25. Taxis are conveniently located outside Terminals 1 and 2.
❶ 02203-404 001 Ⓦ www.koeln-bonn-airport.de

By rail

Cologne's main train station, the Dom/Hbf, is the arrival station for most visitors, and its doors bring you out in front of the magnificent cathedral. The main corridor, from which platforms are reached up flights of stairs, is the Colonnaden shopping centre with a huge range of food outlets and shops. If you need to reach another part of town, the underground (U-Bahn) entrance is to the left of the main door and there are taxi ranks outside both entrances. An information desk faces the front door, underneath the departures board.

By road

The city's bus station lurks behind Dom/Hbf and has little in the way of facilities, apart from a ticket office, but it is right in the centre of town. For journeys to other parts of Cologne hop in a taxi in front of the train station or walk through the Colonnaden to catch the U-Bahn.

It is best to avoid driving into Cologne, because the roads are congested, poorly signposted and there are many one-way streets, making it easy to get lost. Parking in the city centre can also be difficult and expensive, and if you are caught parked illegally there is a fine of at least €30.

If you are arriving by car familiarise yourself with the main streets beforehand. The city is enclosed by several ring roads, running from the Rhine bank in the north round to the river again in the south.

Straight streets run out to this semi-circle like spokes from the city centre.

FINDING YOUR FEET

Cologne's old town is a busy place, but the pace of life is relaxed. The local people are well-known for their outgoing nature and are happy to help tourists. This is also a safe city with a low crime rate, although pickpockets do operate in busy areas around the cathedral, so keep any valuables safe. Most of the main shopping and tourist streets are closed to traffic, but it is worth remembering that Germans drive on the right and that trams run along some streets too. Cyclists are probably more of a hazard, particularly around the ring road, where parallel white lines on the pavement mark the busy cycle lane, which pedestrians should steer clear of.

ORIENTATION

On-foot navigation round Cologne is easy, because the cathedral towers are visible from almost everywhere and are the perfect landmark to head for. There are also plenty of large maps located around the tourist areas and U-Bahn stations.

The narrow streets of the old town between the cathedral and Heumarkt run gently downhill to the river. All the main shopping areas, Hohe Strasse, Schildergasse and the square at Neumarkt, are easily recognisable pedestrian streets that will direct you back to the old town or out to the ring road. The size of the ring road and its volume of traffic make it unmistakable, so you will not cross it unless you mean to. The medieval gate in the square at Rudolfplatz is another landmark you can't miss. .

The maps in this book are up to date and show all the main sights and streets in each area, but many of the restaurants, clubs and shops that we list are on smaller streets for which you will need a larger street plan. If you are planning to stay in Cologne for longer than a couple of days, it's a good idea to acquire a detailed map of the city, preferably one with a street index, from a local newsstand or bookshop or from the tourist office.

GETTING AROUND

By far the best way of exploring the city and surrounding towns is on the state-wide integrated bus, tram and U-Bahn (underground) network. The routes are simple to navigate, each vehicle clearly displays its line number and there are announcements for each

---

IF YOU GET LOST, TRY ...

Excuse me, do you speak English?
Entschuldigen Sie, sprechen Sie Englisch?
Entshuldigen zee, shprekhen zee english?

Excuse me, is this the right way to the old town/the city centre/the tourist office/the station/the bus station?
Entschuldigung, geht es hier zur Altstadt/zur Stadtmitte/ zur Touristeninformation/zum Bahnhof/zum Busbahnhof?
Entshuldeegoong, gayt es here tsoor altshtat/tsoor shtatmitter/ tsoor Touristeninformation/tsoom baanhof/tsoom busbaanhof?

Can you point to it on my map?
Können Sie es mir bitte auf der Karte zeigen?
Kernen see es meer bitter owf der kaarte tsygen?

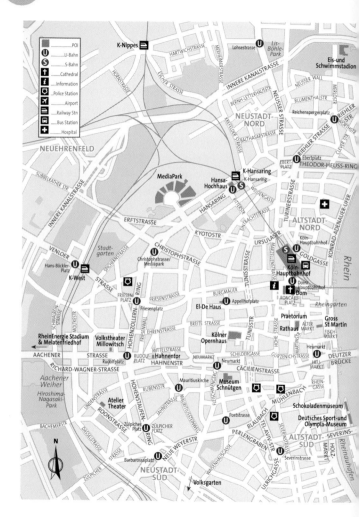

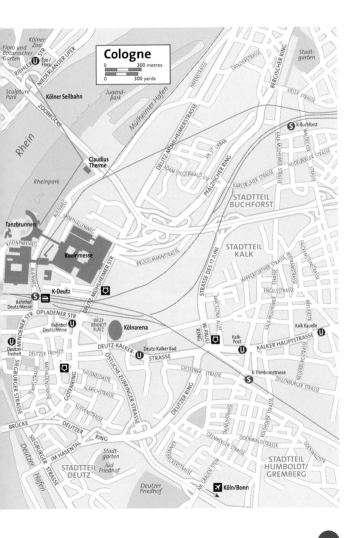

stop. Tickets can be purchased from machines on stations and in trams, or from station kiosks and must be validated (stamped) when you board.

If you are only travelling a short distance, buy a *Kurzstreckenticket* (short-trip ticket), which is valid for four stops. A single trip (1b) ticket will take you anywhere in the city and is valid for 90 minutes (though you can only use in one direction of travel). A cheap option is the *Tagesticket* (day ticket) for Cologne, which lasts until 03.00 the next day.

For those travelling in a group, a five-person *Tagesticket 5 Personen* is the way to go. It's cheaper than buying two single day tickets, but you can only travel after 09.00 on weekdays. For travel outside the city, the tram/bus/underground transport network is often cheaper

◆ *You're never far away from a tram in Cologne*

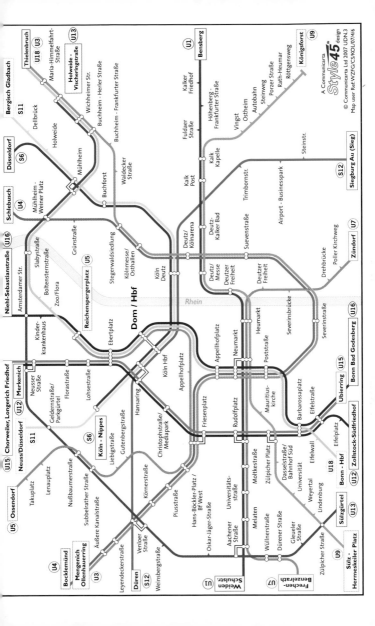

(although slower) than using the train. A 2b CityPlus ticket will take you all the way to Brühl or Bonn. ☏ 24-hour ticket and timetable info 01803 504 030 (9 cents/min) ⓦ www.vrsinfo.de

Licensed taxis usually come in the form of cream-coloured Mercedes and are easy to find day and night at the city's numerous taxi ranks or can be hailed when their light indicates that they are free. There is a minimum charge of €3, and the fares can tick up quite fast, so it might be wise to ask the driver how much the trip will cost before setting off. ☏ 0221-19410 or 0221-2882 ⓦ www.taxiruf.de

CAR HIRE

It is only worthwhile hiring a car if you are heading out of town to explore and there are plenty of rental companies at Köln/Bonn Airport, the main railway station and around town. Pre-booking via your chosen airline's affiliates should secure you reduced rates.

Avis ⓐ 29 Clemensstr. (near Neumarkt) ☏ 0221-234 333
ⓐ Dom/Hauptbahnhof ☏ 0221-913 0063
ⓐ Köln/Bonn Airport ☏ 02203-402 343

Europcar ⓐ 26 Christophstr. ☏ 0221-912 6010
ⓐ Dom/Hauptbahnhof, Trankgasse 11 ☏ 0221-139 2748
ⓐ Köln/Bonn Airport, Mietwagencenter ☏ 02203-955 880

▶ *Cologne's streets are a mix of architectural styles*

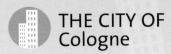

The Altstadt (Old town)

Every trip to Cologne should start in the old town, which sits on the banks of the Rhine, between the impressive cathedral and Heumarkt square. Packed with character and culture, street life and nightlife, it has enough to keep the most energetic sightseer busy and amply fed and watered. The area is largely pedestrianised, so it is easy to explore the maze of cobbled streets on foot and there is no danger of getting lost with the cathedral towers to use as a landmark. Well served by public transport, the old town has the main railway and U-Bahn station (Dom/Hauptbahnhof) right at its centre.

SIGHTS & ATTRACTIONS

The old town is a great place to discover on foot and, while there are many world-class galleries and museums to visit, spare some time for sitting with a coffee or a *Kölsch* and soaking up the relaxed atmosphere. Wandering from the cathedral to the cobbled square of Alter Markt, with its view of the town hall and busy street cafés and *Brauhäuser*, will take less than 20 minutes. From here you can wind your way through cobbled streets towards the river until you reach the colourful old town houses in Fischmarkt, built between the 14th and 17th centuries, overlooked by the church tower of Gross St Martin. If the river-view cafés here don't tempt you to sit down, then continue along the river and make your way onto either the railway or road bridge for excellent views back to the old town and along the Rhine.

Cologne is well used to tourists and any warm day will find the square beneath the cathedral's façade full of street artists and performers, whose favourite trick is to play a statue, only to leap forward and surprise unsuspecting passers-by. Small groups of

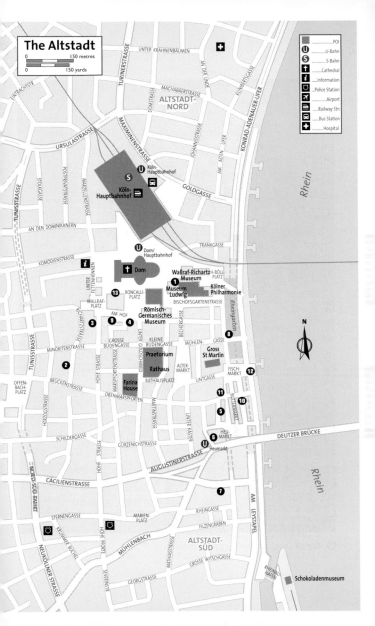

The Altstadt

0 — 150 metres
0 — 150 yards

POI
Ⓤ .....U-Bahn
Ⓢ .....S-Bahn
✝ .....Cathedral
𝒊 .....Information
⊙ .....Police Station
✈ .....Airport
🚆 .....Railway Stn
🚌 .....Bus Station
✚ .....Hospital

◒ Stained glass windows in Cologne's cathedral

musicians also perform in the pedestrian areas around the cathedral, as close to the appreciative audiences of outdoor drinkers and diners as they can get. In December this square also plays host to one of the city's intensely festive Christmas markets.

Dom (Cologne Cathedral)

Testament to the fact that it is impossible to ignore the looming presence of the city's cathedral are the two million visitors who pass through its doors each year, making it Germany's most-visited attraction. This masterpiece of high Gothic architecture has been at the heart of Cologne since its construction began in 1248, but took an incredible 632 years to complete. Work stopped in 1560 and only restarted in the 19th century, when a revival of the Gothic style rekindled interest in the building. When it was finished in 1880, the two 157 m (480 ft) high towers made it the tallest building in the world, until the construction of the Eiffel Tower nine years later. In 1996 the cathedral was designated a world heritage site by UNESCO and remains a powerful religious and architectural focal point for the city.

Fabulous views of the cathedral can be found all over the city, but nothing beats the impact that the blackened stone structure has from the doors of the main rail station, which is at a lower level. From here the spires appear never-ending and there are always tourists struggling to fit their friends and the building into the same photograph. Entering the cathedral through a huge door, which is completely dwarfed by the vast façade, is suitably humbling but does little to prepare the visitor for the scale of the vaulted nave.

Many artworks reside in the cathedral, including a 15th-century altar painting of the city's patron saints and the luminous shrine of the Magi, crafted by German goldsmiths around 1200 and reputed to contain the bones of the Nativity's three kings. More of the cathedral's ecclesiastical riches are on display in the vaulted treasure chamber on the north side of the chancel. The swallow's nest organ, seemingly precariously hanging on the wall of the central nave since 1998, also deserves a moment's contemplation when you realise it weighs 30 tons.

Perhaps one of the best ways to orientate yourself in Cologne (or disorientate yourself if you do not enjoy spiral staircases) is to climb the 509 steps to an observation platform in one of the towers. Although the stairs are in good condition they are only recommended for the fit and fearless, because they can be hot and crowded with people going down as well as up. Whether or not you need a rest, take a break about halfway up to see the bells, one of which is the largest free-swinging bell in the world. Once at the top, if the weather is clear, a panorama of Cologne and the Rhine stretches out beneath you and you can try to spot a good *Brauhaus* to visit for a well-earned *Kölsch* after your descent.

Cathedral ❶ For information about tours (which are usually held in German), call 0221-9258 4730 between 10.00–12.00 and 13.00–15.00 Ⓦ www.koelner-dom.de Ⓛ 06.00–19.30, no viewing during services
Treasure chamber Ⓛ 10.00–18.00 **Tower ascent** Ⓛ 09.00–16.00 Nov–Feb, 09.00–17.00 Mar, Apr & Oct, 09.00–18.00 May–Sept
Ⓝ Train/U-Bahn/Bus: Dom/Hbf. Admission charge

Gross St Martin (Great St Martin's Church)

Almost standing in the cathedral's shadow is Gross St Martin, one of Cologne's 12 Romanesque churches. Built in the 12th and 13th centuries this, like the other churches, was badly damaged during the World War II, but had been lovingly repaired by 1963. Its beautiful tower and steeple, flanked by four smaller towers, are hard to miss from the Fischmarkt, where they look out onto the river from behind the square's cafés. Although it is an impressive space, the interior of the church is disconcertingly bare, so may only really appeal to religious visitors and those of an architectural persuasion. ● 10.00–12.00, 15.00–17.00 Tues–Fri, 10.00–12.30, 13.30–17.00 Sat, 14.00–16.00 Sun ⊚ Train/U-Bahn: Dom/Hbf; bus: Rathaus; tram: Heumarkt.

Rathaus (Town Hall)

It is well worth taking some time to look round Rathausplatz, especially if you are planning a visit to the Wallraf-Richartz Museum, which takes up one side of the leafy square. The benches shaded by trees provide a welcome rest for tired feet and a great view of Cologne's historic town hall. Its 15th-century church-like tower and wonderful 16th-century loggia are evidence of the city's affluent past and contrast with the 20th-century section of the complex, built after bomb damage. Tours can be booked through the Cologne Tourist Board (see page 152). The foundations of the Praetorium (Roman governor's palace) can also be seen underneath the town hall (see page 66). In the centre of the square, protected by a glass roof that the curious can peer through, is the Mikwe. This is an excavation of a medieval Jewish ritual bath dating from about 1170 and has a steep staircase leading down about 15m to a pool. ❸ Rathauspl. (near Alter Markt) ⊚ U-Bahn: Dom/Hbf, Heumarkt; bus: 132 to Rathaus

CULTURE

Cologne prides itself on being a city of art and culture, and many of its major galleries, museums and venues can be found in the old town. These exhibitions are all housed in modern, purpose-built venues, where there is plenty of space, light and air. Most museums have cloakrooms, and visitors are required to leave bulky bags in lockers. All of Cologne's museums are closed on Mondays.

Farina House

The home of the world's oldest eau de cologne factory named after perfumer Giovanni Maria Farina, who invented the original Cologne water in 1709. The museum looks at the history of this city's famous perfume and the Farina family. It's very popular with tourists and can get a little crowded. The factory sells one of the two brands of eau de cologne available in the city today; the other is the better-known 4711 (see pages 86–7). ❷ Obenmarspforten 21 ❶ 0221-3998 9941 ⓦ www.farinagegenueber.de ❺ 11.00–18.00 Mon–Sat ❻ U-Bahn: Heumarkt. Admission charge

Kölner Philharmonie (Philharmonic Hall)

Located in the city centre, just down the steps from Museum Ludwig, is one of Cologne's finest music venues. Opened in 1986, the Philharmonic Hall hosts a huge variety of concerts from traditional and modern classical performances to jazz, folk and pop music. Concerts are held almost daily and there are often as many as three a day on Sundays and public holidays. The design of the concert hall itself is based on an amphitheatre, with the stage almost in the centre of the space, affording the audience uninterrupted views of the orchestra. Concert listings can be found on the website or in the Köln Musik ticket office, next door to the Römisch-Germanisches Museum. ❷ Bischofgartenstr. 1 ❶ 0221-204 080 ⓦ www.koelner-philharmonie.de ❻ Train/Bus & U-Bahn: Dom/Hbf

Museum Ludwig

An art gallery rather than a museum, this fabulously light and airy building behind the cathedral houses the city's collection of 20th- and 21st-century art. Spread over four floors are icons of American Pop Art, masterpieces of German Expressionism, Surrealism, Russian

⏷ *The Renaissance façade of the Rathaus*

avant-garde and contemporary art. The first-floor galleries boast a collection of Picasso paintings and sculpture, as well as works by Dalí and Magritte. Special exhibitions, which change regularly, are displayed on the floor below the entrance hall and admission to them is included in the entrance fee. An English audio-guide is available at the ticket desk for €3, but for those who do not need in-depth analysis all exhibits are labelled in German and English. ⓐ Bischofsgartenstr. 1 ⓣ 0221-26165 ⓦ www.museenkoeln.de/museum-ludwig ⓛ 10.00–18.00 Tues–Sun, 10.00–22.00 first Fri of the month ⓝ Train/Bus & U-Bahn: Dom/Hbf. Admission charge

Römisch-Germanisches Museum (Roman-Germanic Museum)

Also next door to the cathedral, this museum is a must for anyone with even the slightest interest in Roman history. Go downstairs first to view the impressive Dionysius mosaic, which was found in the city in 1941 during excavations for an air-raid shelter. Exhibits cover every

---

PRAETORIUM EXCAVATIONS

Another taste of Roman influence on life in Cologne can be found beneath the Rathaus (town hall), where the foundations of the 1st–4th-century AD Roman governor's palace are preserved. In its time this was the most important building on the Rhine and is now complemented with an exhibition of Roman monuments and art, along with a well-preserved section of a Roman sewer that visitors can walk through, marvelling at the skills of the ancient engineers. ⓐ Entrance: Kleine Budengasse ⓛ 10.00–17.00 Tues–Sun ⓝ Bus: Rathaus or Gürzenich; tram: Heumarkt. Admission charge

aspect of Roman life, from shoes and jewellery to amphorae and bridge foundations. Roman Colonia was a centre for glass production, famous for its exquisite pieces with 'snake thread' decoration, and the volume of pristine local finds on display is fascinating. Although English labelling is not comprehensive, there is enough information available to understand the exhibits and room for some fun filling in the gaps for yourself. ⓐ Roncallipl. 4 ⓣ 0221-2212 4438 ⓦ www.museenkoeln.de/roemisch-germanisches-museum ⓛ 10.00–17.00 Tues–Sun ⓝ Train/bus/U-Bahn: Dom/Hbf. Admission charge

Wallraf-Richartz Museum/Fondation Corboud

This new building, the sister gallery to Museum Ludwig, opened in 2001 and is home to Western painting from the 13th to the 19th centuries, and should cater to most tastes. The medieval paintings assembled on the second floor are astonishingly vibrant and many of them are from Cologne. In fact, *The Martyrdom of St Ursula at the City of Cologne* (1411) is the earliest identifiable depiction of the city. The third floor boasts a huge range of 17th-century Dutch and Flemish paintings, including pieces by Rembrandt, Rubens and Van Dyck, while the fifth floor is reserved for 18th- and 19th-century art. Here, the ever-popular Impressionists are represented by Renoir, Monet and Sisley, while paintings by Van Gogh, Cèzanne and Munch are the icing on the cake. An English audio-guide is available from the information desk for €2.50, although there is labelling in English throughout the galleries. Widely publicised temporary exhibitions are also held in the gallery and can be visited on payment of an additional fee. ⓐ Martinstr. 39 ⓣ 0221-2212 1119 ⓦ www.museenkoeln.de/wallraf-richartz-museum ⓛ 10.00–20.00 Tues, 10.00–18.00 Wed–Fri, 11.00–18.00 Sat & Sun ⓝ Bus: Rathaus, Gürzenich; tram: Heumarkt. Admission charge

THE CITY

RETAIL THERAPY

For serious shoppers the short walk to nearby Hohe Strasse
(see page 81) would probably be worthwhile, but if it is a kitsch
memento of your visit you need then the old town is the right
place to find it. The brazen souvenir outlets in the streets
surrounding the cathedral, selling postcards and models of the
famous building, could not contrast more with the upmarket
boutiques nearby, nestled next to the Dom Hotel. There is also
a shopping centre in the main railway station, with everything
from bookshops to pharmacies.

SOUVENIR SHOPS

CCAA Glasgalerie A great stop for stylish souvenirs, this gallery
sells original reproductions of Roman glass artefacts found in
the Cologne area, as well as modern creations by contemporary
artists. ⓐ Auf dem Berlich 30 ⓣ 0221-257 6191 ⓦ www.ccaa.de
ⓛ 10.00–13.00, 14.00–18.00 Tues–Fri, 10.00–16.00 Sat, closed Mon
ⓝ U-Bahn: Appellhofplatz

Gaffel Kölsch Shop Wedged between two *Brauhäuser* is a shop
selling everything you need to set up your own *Brauhaus* at home,
including *Stangen*, the small straight-sided glasses. ⓐ Alter Markt 24
ⓣ 0221-257 7818 ⓦ www.gaffel.de ⓛ 11.00–19.00 Tues–Fri,
10.00–18.00 Sat ⓝ U-Bahn: Heumarkt

BOUTIQUES

Chopard Boutique Exclusive jewellery and watches in a classically
styled store. ⓐ Domkloster 2 ⓣ 0221-925 7990 ⓛ 10.00–19.00
Mon–Fri, 10.30–19.00 Sat, closed Sun ⓝ Train/Tram/U-Bahn: Dom/Hbf

Louis Vuitton Luxurious surroundings and excellent service will please fans of this top-quality brand of luggage and shoes. ⓐ Domkloster 2 ⓣ 0221-257 6828 ⓦ www.louisvuitton.com ⓛ 10.00–19.00 Mon–Fri, 10.00–18.00 Sat, closed Sun ⓝ Train/Tram/U-Bahn: Dom/Hbf

Rhine Gold Individually designed jewellery, made by local goldsmiths. ⓐ Frankenwerft 11 ⓣ 0221-257 8708 ⓛ 10.00–18.30 Tues–Fri, 10.00–18.00 Sat; closed Sun and Mon ⓝ U-Bahn: Heumarkt

TAKING A BREAK

Whatever your tonic – ice cream, coffee, *Kölsch* – there are plenty of places in the old town to sit down and recharge. Most *Brauhäuser* (see pages 70–2) serve drinks and food throughout the day, as do the following establishments if you fancy something different.

Café Böll £ ❶ On the ground floor of the Wallraf-Richartz Museum, this stylish spot serves good espressos, pastries and salad dishes. ⓐ Martinstr. 39 ⓣ 0221-283 5256 ⓛ 09.30–20.00 Tues–Sat, 10.30–20.00 Sun, closed Mon ⓝ U-Bahn: Heumarkt

Café Valentin £ ❷ This lovely café with an outdoor terrace is a great place for coffee and cake, and typical German snacks. Favourites include tasty bacon pancakes or baked potatoes with quark. ⓐ Ludwigstrasse 11 ⓣ 0221-9589 9877 ⓛ 09.00–18.30 Mon–Fri, 09.00–18.00 Sat ⓝ Train/Tram/U-Bahn: Dom/Hbf

Eis-Café Sagui £ ❸ This excellent ice cream parlour is tucked round the corner from the Dom Hotel and serves ridiculously indulgent sundaes, as well as coffee, with ruthless efficiency.

ⓐ Hohe Str. 164–8 ❶ 0221-258 0440 ⓛ 09.30-23.00 (closes later in summer), closed Sun Ⓝ U-Bahn: Heumarkt

Raffaello £ ❹ Another good ice cream parlour, with views of the cathedral, Raffaello excels at tall sundaes loaded with fruit. ⓐ Am Hof 28 ❶ 0221-420 7960 ⓛ 09.30–23.30 Apr–Oct, 09.30–22.30 Nov–Mar Ⓝ Train/Tram/U-Bahn: Dom/Hbf

AFTER DARK

BRAUHÄUSER (BREWERY PUBS)
Brauerei zum Pfaffen £ ❺ Housed in the beautiful orange building on the corner of Heumarkt, with an interior filled with carved wood and stained glass. Serves delicious Pfaffen *Kölsch* and substantial regional dishes. ⓐ Heumarkt 62 ❶ 0221-257 7765 ⓦ www.max-paeffgen.de ⓛ 11.00–24.00 Tues–Sun, closed Mon; warm dishes stop an hour before closing Ⓝ U-Bahn: Heumarkt

Haus Zims £ ❻ One of the few survivors of wartime bombing, this building dates from 1568 and its small windows and wood panelling make for a cosy feel inside. Good meat and mushroom-based dishes go down well with the Gilden *Kölsch*. ⓐ Heumarkt 77 ❶ 0221-258 1261 ⓛ 10.00–24.00 Ⓝ U-Bahn: Heumarkt

Malzmühle £ ❼ As well as being famous for its local brew, this *Brauhaus* also serves traditional Cologne fare with a heavy emphasis on meat. Can get packed with locals and tourists. ⓐ Heumarkt 6 ❶ 0221-210 117 ⓦ www.muehlenkoelsch.de ⓛ 10.00–24.00 Mon–Sat, 11–24.00 Sun Ⓝ U-Bahn: Heumarkt

Peters Brauhaus £ ❶ Friendly, traditional tavern that serves
good food and a range of schnapps as well as *Kölsch*. The huge
stained-glass ceiling light is also worth a look. ⓐ Mühlengasse 1
❶ 0221-257 3950 ⓦ www.peters-brauhaus.de ❶ 11.30–00.30
Ⓝ Train/Tram/U-Bahn: Dom/Hbf

🔺 *As evening falls the crowds make for the* Brauhäuser

Früh am Dom ££ ❾ A popular place from breakfast until late, with a vaulted cellar bar, a traditional *Brauhaus* and more subdued first-floor restaurant, as well as outside tables. Credit cards accepted in restaurant. ⓐ Am Hof 12–18 ⓣ 0221-261 3211 Ⓦ www.frueh.de Ⓛ *Brauhaus*: 08.00–24.00, Restaurant: 12.00–24.00 Ⓝ Train/Tram/U-Bahn: Dom/Hbf

RESTAURANTS

Restaurant Beirut £ ❿ Centrally placed but relatively tourist-free, this restaurant serves tasty Lebanese specialities. Every meal comes with a smile and a complimentary peppermint tea. ⓐ Buttermarkt 3 ⓣ 0221-258 1539 Ⓛ 12.00–23.30 Mon–Sun Ⓝ U-Bahn: Heumarkt

Ristorante da Pino £ ⓫ A reasonably priced Italian restaurant that cooks up tasty pizza, antipasti, meat and fish dishes from lunch until late. Seating outside in a quiet square. ⓐ Salzgasse 4 ⓣ 0221-257 7769 Ⓦ www.restaurantdapino.de Ⓛ 11.00–01.00 Ⓝ U-Bahn: Heumarkt

Das Kleine Stapelhäusen ££ ⓬ Its traditional decor, Rhine-side setting, top-notch German food and good wine list make this a great choice for lunch or dinner. ⓐ Fischmarkt 1–3 ⓣ 0221-257 7862 Ⓛ 11.30–23.30 Ⓝ U-Bahn: Heumarkt

Le Merou £££ ⓭ This is primarily a seafood restaurant, with exquisite lobster and oyster specialities and an extensive wine list. ⓐ Dom Hotel, Domkloster 2a ⓣ 0221-20240 Ⓛ 12.00–23.00 Ⓝ Train/Tram/U-Bahn: Dom/Hbf

BARS

Barney Valley's Irish Pub A small bar, cluttered with Irish ephemera, playing loud music and pouring stouts and whiskies as well as *Kölsch*.

🅐 Kleine Budengasse 7–9 ☎ 0221-257 0820 🕐 11.00–02.00 Sun–Thur, 11.00–23.00 Fri & Sat Ⓝ Train/Tram/U-Bahn: Dom/Hbf

Bier Museum Not as staid as it sounds: a lively bar, playing cheesy music and, unusually for Cologne, offering 18 beers on tap, including Guinness. 🅐 Buttermarkt 39 ☎ 0221-257 7802 🕐 14.00–03.00 Ⓝ U-Bahn: Heumarkt

Papa Joe's Jazzlokal Relax with a *Kölsch* in suitably dingy surroundings and listen to live jazz daily. 🅐 Buttermarkt 37 ☎ 0221-257 7931 🅦 www.papajoes.de 🕐 20.00–03.00 Mon–Sat, 16.00–03.00 Sun Ⓝ U-Bahn: Heumarkt

Sonderbar One of the few trendy bars in the old town, with regular DJs, stylish lighting and a huge mirrorball. 🅐 Lintgasse 28 🅦 www.sonderbar-koeln.de 🕐 19.00–02.00 Sun–Thur, 19.00–03.00 Fri & Sat Ⓝ U-Bahn: Heumarkt

Taberna Flamenca A friendly Spanish restaurant and bar that's a meeting place for Spaniards and Latinos. Good food and live music every evening (except Monday) from 21.00. 🅐 Salzgasse 8 ☎ 0221-942 4352 🅦 www.taberna-flamenca.net 🕐 19.00–05.00 Tues–Sun, closed Mon

CLUBS

Alter Wartesaal A stylish art deco restaurant, bar and club, playing mainly R&B, funk and soul, set in the old waiting rooms of the former train station. Popular with Cologne's thriving artist scene. Also hosts gay and lesbian parties. 🅐 Johannisstr. 11 ☎ 0221-912 8850 🅦 www.wartesaal.de 🕐 Bar 18.00–02.00, club hours depend on the event Ⓝ Train/Tram/U-Bahn: Dom/Hbf

The Innenstadt (city centre)

When you've had your fill of culture and *Kölsch* in the old town, head for Cologne's busiest shopping streets, only a few minutes' walk from the Rhine, beginning on crowded Hohe Strasse, along Schildergasse, and on to the tram and U-Bahn hub at Neumarkt.

This is not the most visually attractive part of the city, but serious shoppers will only have eyes for the vast range of consumables on offer, and the fact that the bulk of the streets are pedestrianised makes it an enjoyable place to browse. Hohe Strasse and Schildergasse hold few surprises as they're full of international chain stores, although some of the German brand names will be new to tourists. Enclosed shopping centres off Neumarkt and Appellhofplatz are good places to aim for if it's raining, as are the huge department stores on Schildergasse.

Not much happens in the city centre in the evening, as it sits between the much livelier old town and the cooler local haunts near the ring road. It is, however, safe to walk in, and if you're passing through or are tired after a long day of retail therapy there are a few bars worth stopping off at.

SIGHTS & ATTRACTIONS

If you need a break from all the clothes and shoes, or have companions who don't want to shop, there are several attractions in this part of town that will keep anyone entertained for a few hours. By far the most popular is the Chocolate Museum, perched right on the bank of the Rhine, which is just a pleasant, well-signposted walk or short tram-ride away.

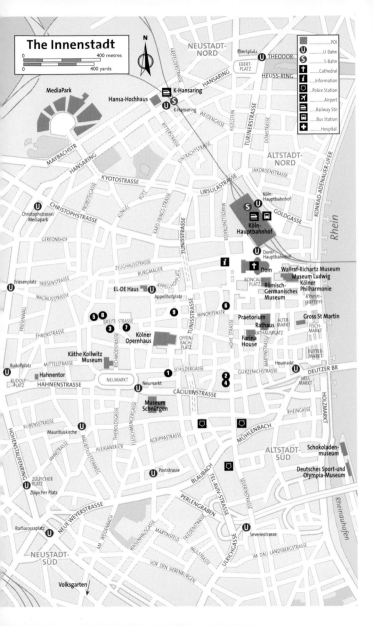

The Innenstadt

N

0 — 400 metres
0 — 400 yards

POI
U ...U Bahn
S ...S-Bahn
✝ ...Cathedral
i ...Information
✕ ...Police Station
✈ ...Airport
🚂 ...Railway Stn
🚌 ...Bus Station
✚ ...Hospital

MediaPark

NEUSTADT-NORD

Eberplatz

U THEODOR-
HEUSS-RING

Hansa-Hochhaus

S K-Hansaring
U K-Hansaring

MAYBACHSTR

HANSARING

KYOTOSTRASSE

ALTSTADT-NORD

JAKORDENSTRASSE

URSULASTRASSE

Köln-Hauptbahnhof

U Christophstrasse/
Mediapark

CHRISTOPHSTRASSE

GEREONSHOF

GOLDGASSE

S **U**
Köln-Hauptbahnhof

Rhein

KONRAD-ADENAUER-UFER

U Friesenplatz   FRIESENSTRASSE

MAGNUSSTRASSE

ZEUGHAUSSTRASSE

BURGMAUER

U Dom/
Hauptbahnhof

i

✝ Dom

Wallraf-Richartz Museum
Museum Ludwig
Kölner Philharmonie

RONCALLI
PLATZ

Römisch-
Germanisches
Museum

Rhein-
garten

EL-DE Haus **U**
Appellhofplatz

❾

APPELLHOFPLATZ

❻

Praetorium
Rathaus

Gross St Martin

FISCH-
MARKT

❺ **❽** BREITE STRASSE
❸ **❼**
Kölner
Opernhaus

Farina
House

Heumarkt

BUTTER-
MARKT

Käthe Kollwitz
Museum

OFFEN-
BACH
PLATZ

SCHILDERGASSE

❷
❹

GÜRZENICHSTRASSE

DEUTZER BR

U
Rudolfplatz

MITTELSTRASSE

Hahnentor

NEUMARKT

U Neumarkt

CÄCILIENSTRASSE

HELL-
MARKT

RUDOLF
PLATZ

HAHNENSTRASSE

❶

HOLZMARKT

Museum
Schnütgen

RHEINGASSE

RUBENSSTRASSE

Mauritiuskirche

AGRIPPASTRASSE

MÜHLENBACH

ALTSTADT-
SÜD

Schokoladen-
museum

ALEXIANERSTR

U Poststrasse

BLAUBACH

Deutsches Sport- und
Olympia-Museum

U
ZÜLPICHER
PLATZ
Zülpicher Platz

PERLENGRABEN

Rheinauhafen

HOHENSTAUFENRING

NEUE WEYERSTRASSE

Barbarossaplatz

U Severinstrasse

NEUSTADT-
SÜD

VOR DEN SIEBENBURGEN

IM DALI LANDSBERGSTRASSE

Volksgarten

Deutsches Sport & Olympia Museum
(German Sport & Olympic Museum)

This museum charts the development of sports through the ages,
from the athletes of ancient Greece to the ever-changing technology
of today's Formula 1 cars. A treasure trove for sports fanatics, the
museum is full of memorabilia, including examples of the kit and
equipment that have helped champions to victory. There are also
displays focusing on the German Olympic games held in Berlin in
1936 and Munich in 1972. All of the main explanations are in English
as well as German and most of the exhibits themselves need little
introduction. If you have some extra energy to burn off you can try
your hand at racing a cycle through a wind tunnel, throwing your
best right hook at punch bags in a boxing ring, or squeezing into

🔺 *The Formula 1 exhibition at the Sport Museum is popular with kids*

a four-man bobsleigh. Another highlight could be a game of football on Cologne's highest sports field on the museum's roof. 🄰 Rheinauhafen 1 🌐 0221-336 090 🌐 www.sportmuseum.info 🕐 10.00–18.00 Tues–Fri, 11.00–19.00 Sat & Sun, closed Mon 🄽 Tram: Heumarkt; U-Bahn: Severinstr. Admission charge

Museum Schnütgen

A welcome oasis of calm after the tourist frenzy of the cathedral. The museum holds one of Europe's most important medieval religious collections, covering 1,000 years of art history from the early Middle Ages to the end of the Baroque period. And it's all displayed in the original setting of Cäcilienkirche (St Cecilia's), a Romanesque church dating back to the tenth century. Some 700 items are on show, including carvings in wood, stone and ivory, as well as tapestries and glasswork. A new cultural centre is being built onto the entrance of the church, which will greatly extend the exhibition space when completed in 2009. 🄰 Cäcilienstr. 29 ☎ 0221-2212 3620 🌐 www.museenkoeln.de/museum-schnuetgen 🕐 10.00–17.00 Tues–Fri, 11.00–17.00 Sat & Sun, closed Mon ☎ Tram/Bus/U-Bahn: Neumarkt. Admission charge

Schokoladenmuseum (Imhoff-Stollwerck-Museum) (Chocolate Museum)

Since 2000, this former customs office has been the place for chocoholics of every age to discover the history of their favourite treat and try a few samples – in the name of research, of course.

After walking through a grove of cacao trees in the tropical greenhouse, you can go on to see how the raw cacao is roasted, melted, moulded and packaged by following a real production line, all clearly explained in English. Once you've got to grips with that, find out how truffles and novelty shapes are created and delve into chocolate's long history. If you are flagging after all this hard work, a sip from the chocolate fountain might keep you going long enough to reach the shop, which is overflowing with chocolate goodies to take home. It would be easy to while away a few hours here, particularly if you stop for coffee or lunch in the glass-fronted café and take in the views of the Rhine from the roof. ⓐ Rheinauhafen 1a ⓣ 0221-9318 8860 ⓦ www.schokoladenmuseum.de ⓛ 10.00–17.00 Tues–Fri, 11.00–18.00 Sat & Sun, closed Mon ⓝ Tram: Heumarkt; U-Bahn: Severinstr. Admission charge

CULTURE

Art, music and history can all be found in the city centre at three venues that could not be more different.

EL-DE Haus

Cologne's former Gestapo headquarters now house the National Socialist Documentation Centre along with a museum tracing the history of the Nazi party in the city. The ten torture chambers and cells with their graffiti from prisoners on their way to death camps are at the centre of the exhibition. In 2006, EL-DE Haus was given the prestigious 'Best in Heritage' award by the European Heritage Association. Incidentally, the museum's name comes from the initials of Leopold Dahmen, who ran the jewellery shop in the building when it was seized by the Nazis in 1934. ⓐ Appellhofpl. 23–25 ⓣ 0221-2212 6331 ⓦ www.museenkoeln.de/ns-dok ⓛ 10.00–16.00 Tues–Fri, 11.00–16.00 Sat & Sun, closed Mon ⓝ Tram/U-Bahn: Appellhof. Admission charge

ⓞ *Dip into the chocolate fountain!*

THE INNENSTADT (CITY CENTRE)

🔺 *A performance of* Rigoletto *at the Opera House*

Käthe Kollwitz Museum

This gallery on the upper level of the Neumarkt Passage shopping arcade holds the largest collection of Kollwitz's often dark and emotional drawings, prints, posters and sculptures. One of Germany's most important Expressionist artists of the early 20th century, her work echoes her difficult and tragic life, spent mostly in Berlin. The museum is owned by the Kreissparkasse Köln bank and was opened in 1985. ⓐ Neumarkt 18–24 ⓣ 0221-227 2899 ⓦ www.kollwitz.de ⓣ 10.00–18.00 Tues–Fri, 11.00–18.00 Sat & Sun, closed Mon ⓜ U-Bahn/Tram & Bus: Neumarkt. Admission charge

Kölner Opernhaus (Cologne Opera House)

If all the singing in the *Brauhäuser* has left you yearning for something more refined, a trip to Cologne's famous opera house might be just the ticket. Situated in Germany's largest theatre complex, along with the Schauspielhaus, which hosts modern and classical theatre, and the tiny West End Theater, home to modern productions, the opera house can seat an audience of 1,300. Every year it has a varied repertoire of 20th-century and classical works and ballet features heavily, too. Tickets are also available through Köln Ticket (see page 31). ⓐ Offenbachpl. ❶ 0221-2212 8400 ⓦ www.buehnenkoeln.de Box office 🕐 10.00–19.30 Mon–Fri, 11.00–19.30 Sat, closed Sun Ⓝ U-Bahn: Appellhofplatz

RETAIL THERAPY

You could easily spend a day exploring the city centre's shops and department stores, so get your walking shoes on (or make the Birkenstock shop first on your list) and get started. All stores are closed on Sundays, and many of the larger shops stay open longer on Fridays.

HOHE STRASSE

Germany's first pedestrian shopping street is not Cologne's most glamorous, but is packed with international clothing brands such as H&M, Zara and Mango, alongside The Body Shop, Foot Locker and various fast-food giants.

Galeria Kaufhof You can't miss this massive department store. It sells anything you could ever want, but is particularly good for fashion, cosmetics and jewellery. The basement food hall is also a treat, crammed with chocolate, deli counters, fresh produce and a huge selection of wine and beer. ⓐ Hohe Str. 41–53 ⓦ www.galeria-kaufhof.de 🕐 09.30–20.00 Mon–Thur, 09.30–21.00 Fri & Sat, closed Sun Ⓝ U-Bahn: Heumarkt

SCHILDERGASSE

Leading off Hohe Strasse, this is a wider, more attractive thoroughfare, with space for bag-laden shoppers and street cafés. Big stores such as Benetton and C&A vie for your attention, as do international fast-food chains.

Douglas An oasis of beauty products in a lovely, softly lit space. There's occasional live music downstairs next to the coffee bar. ⓐ Schildergasse 39 ⓦ www.douglas.de ⓛ 10.00–20.00 Mon–Thur & Sat, 10.00–21.00 Fri, closed Sun Ⓝ U-Bahn: Heumarkt

Humanic More shoes than you could ever imagine, for men, women and children, over three floors. Also Playstations in the basement and a first-floor café for the easily bored. ⓐ Schildergasse 94–96a ⓦ www.humanic.at ⓛ 10.00–20.00 Mon–Thur & Sat, 10.00–21.00 Fri, closed Sun Ⓝ U-Bahn: Neumarkt

Sport Scheck A gigantic sports superstore on six floors stuffed with sportswear, shoes and equipment for every activity. ⓐ Schildergasse 38 ⓦ www.sportscheck.com ⓛ 10.00–20.00 Mon–Thur & Sat, 10.00–21.00 Fri, closed Sun Ⓝ U-Bahn: Heumarkt

NEUMARKT

The square at the end of Schildergasse, bustling with trams and people heading for the U-Bahn station, is the place to go for under-cover shopping when the weather is bad. The modern glass and steel façade of the Neumarkt Galerie is easy to spot from a distance as there's a giant, upside-down ice cream cone melting over one of its corners, the precise significance of which remains unclear. Ⓝ U-Bahn: Neumarkt

🔺 *Schildergasse is just one of the city's many pedestrianised shopping streets*

NEUMARKT GALERIE

Cologne's largest shopping centre is smart and airy, with a vast range of outlets selling health food, jewellery, clothes, books and shoes. Abundant restaurants, coffee shops and ice cream parlours are an added temptation. Well worth a visit is **Mayersche Buchhandlung**, which holds half a million books, including some in English, on three floors; there's also a large reading area with tables and sockets for laptops. English magazines can also be found on the ground floor. **Sinn Leffer** is yet another giant store selling a massive range of brand-name fashion for men and women, including Tommy Hilfiger, Mexx and Esprit. ❸ Neumarkt 2 ⓦ www.neumarkt-galerie.de ❶ Most shops open 09.30–20.00 Mon–Sat, closed Sun

Daniels Extremely sleek and stylish menswear store stocked with designer gear including Armani, Boss and Ralph Lauren. ❸ Neumarkt 18 ⓦ www.daniels-mode.de ❶ 10.00–20.00 Mon–Sat, closed Sun ⓝ U-Bahn: Neumarkt

Globetrotter With four floors of everything you could ever need in the outdoors, Globetrotter is gear-freak heaven. Try out scuba equipment or a kayak in the pool, test a sleeping bag in the cool room, and check if a jacket is really waterproof in the rain room. An adventure in itself. ❸ Olivenhaindorf Richmodstr. 10 ❶ 0221-277 2880 ⓦ www.globetrotter.de ❶ 10.00–20.00 Mon–Thur & Sat, 10.00–22.00 Fri, closed Sun ⓝ U-Bahn: Neumarkt

◀ *Globetrotter: feel like having a paddle?*

BREITE STRASSE

Parallel to Schildergasse and close to the opera house, this is another relaxed, pedestrianised street with shops selling interior goods, clothes, footwear, jewellery and leather goods.

4711 Haus Just a few steps from Breite Strasse, this beautiful building, rebuilt after the original was destroyed during the war, is home to the

◗ *The home of authentic cologne*

THE INNENSTADT (CITY CENTRE)

famous 4711 eau de cologne in its turquoise bottles. The scent used to be manufactured here by the Mulhens family, but today the site serves as a perfume boutique and exhibition. 🔵 Glockengasse 4711 🌐 www.4711.com 🕐 09.00–19.00 Mon–Fri, 09.30–18.00 Sat, closed Sun 🔵 U-Bahn: Heumarkt

Galerie Karstadt Another of Cologne's huge department stores, with a gourmet supermarket in the basement, a music store on the top floor and everything from books to clothes to cosmetics in between. 🔵 Breite Str. 103 🌐 www.karstadt.de 🕐 10.00–20.00 Mon–Thur & Sat, 10.00–21.00 Fri, closed Sun 🔵 U-Bahn: Appellhofplatz

Heubel Antique and modern furniture, accessories and jewellery. Heaven for browsers. 🔵 Breite Str. 118 🌐 www.heubel.de 🕐 10.00–19.00 Mon–Fri, 10.00–18.00 Sat, closed Sun 🔵 U-Bahn: Appellhofplatz

Maus & Co Dedicated to Germany's most famous TV mouse and filled with soft toys, clothes and endless items featuring the cuddly orange character. 🔵 Breite Str. 6–26 (in the WDR arcade) 🕐 10.00–19.00 Mon–Fri, 10.00–18.00 Sat, closed Sun 🔵 U-Bahn: Appellhofplatz

TAKING A BREAK

Crowds of hungry and thirsty shoppers mean there are many options for drinks and lunch in the city centre. All of the shopping streets are scattered with coffee shops, and the malls and department stores provide plenty of good and varied places to eat, so you don't need to stray far if your retail therapy is set to continue. There are also little market stalls selling fresh fruit on Hohe Strasse, where you could grab something on the go.

Al Cappuccino £ ❶ Serves ice cream and coffee as well as snacks.
ⓐ Schildergasse 98 ❶ 0221-255 558 ⓛ 09.00–22.00, until 23.00 Fri & Sat
Ⓝ U-Bahn: Neumarkt

Sky Beach £ ❷ Relax in a deckchair under palm trees and let the sand
trickle through your toes right in the middle of Cologne. The beach
bar is on the top floor of the Galeria Kaufhof department store (enter
at the P2 car park). ⓐ Galeria Kaufhof, Hohe Str. Ⓦ www.skybeach.de
ⓛ 11.00–late May–Sept Ⓝ U-Bahn: Heumarkt

DEPARTMENT STORES

Galerie Karstadt £ ❸ The store's restaurant is a good choice for lunch,
provided you can make it to the top floor without being distracted.
ⓐ Breite Str. 103 Ⓦ www.karstadt.de ⓛ 10.00–20.00 Mon–Thur & Sat,
10.00–21.00 Fri, closed Sun Ⓝ U-Bahn: Appellhofplatz

Galeria Kaufhof £ ❹ Visit the food hall in the basement of this
department store and take the weight off your feet at the little Italian
café or wine bar, both of which serve good, moderately priced light
lunches. ⓐ Hohe Str. 41–53 Ⓦ www.galeria-kaufhof.de ⓛ 09.30–20.00
Mon–Thur, 09.30–21.00 Fri & Sat, closed Sun Ⓝ U-Bahn: Heumarkt

AFTER DARK

This is not Cologne's party district, so don't expect to find much
more than a few friendly bars. That said, many of the restaurants
geared towards hungry shoppers during the day also stay open into
the evening and might make a welcome change from the busy tourist
spots of the old town. Otherwise, unless you're going to the theatre

or the opera, there is little to keep the visitor in the city centre after the shops have closed.

Bento Box £ ❺ Busy, reasonably priced Japanese sushi and noodle bar, with clean minimalist décor and an open kitchen so you can watch the chefs at work. Further branches at Ubierring 33 and Neusserstr 41. ❷ Breite Str. 116 ❶ 0221-420 7746 ❿ www.bentobox.de ❶ 12.00–22.30 Mon–Sat, closed Sun ❿ U-Bahn: Appellhofplatz

Café Piano £ ❻ On the corner of Hohe Strasse and Minoritenstrasse, this cheerful place serves coffee, ice cream, steaks and *Schnitzel* from early morning onwards. ❷ Minoritenstr. 2 ❶ 0221-257 6659 ❶ 8.00–22.00 ❿ U-Bahn: Appellhofplatz

Bei Bepi ££ ❼ With its ever-changing menu and pasta specialities, this vibrant Italian restaurant remains popular after nearly 40 years. ❷ Breite Str. 85 ❶ 0221-257 6370 ❶ 11.00–23.30 Mon–Sat, closed Sun ❿ U-Bahn: Appellhofplatz

Bier-Esel ££ ❽ This *Brauhaus* serves *Kölsch*, as you might expect, but is also known locally for its good mussel dishes. ❷ Breite Str. 114 ❶ 0221-257 6090 ❶ 10.00–24.00 ❿ U-Bahn: Appellhofplatz

Gaststätte 'La Pad' ££ ❾ A cosy bar, cluttered with heavy, dark furniture and copper pots, that stretches back from a small front on the street. Shared by locals and tourists enjoying *Kölsch* and comforting hot drinks including *Glühwein* (hot spiced wine) and tea with rum. ❷ Breite Str. 32 ❶ 0221-257 8412 ❶ 16.00–01.00 Mon–Sat, closed Sun ❿ U-Bahn: Appellhofplatz

Around the Ringstrassen (ring road)

Once you pass Neumarkt and move through progressively quirkier and cooler shopping streets towards Cologne's ring road, it feels distinctly as if you are stepping off the tourist trail and into the real city where people live and work. Fortunately, because the pace of life in Cologne is so laid-back, the whole area around Zülpicherplatz, Rudolfplatz and Friesenplatz is an ideal place to wander, shop and stop off at cafés during the day, and go clubbing all night. This is the part of town that the students, professionals, artists and media-types frequent, which makes it vibrant, busy and, best of all, a great place to people-watch. Getting there is no problem, as trams run from the old town to Zülpicherplatz and Rudolfplatz as well as around the ring road, and the U-Bahn stops at Friesenplatz.

SIGHTS & ATTRACTIONS

The semi-circle of Cologne's ring road follows the line of the medieval city wall, which was demolished to make way for it. Remnants of the old wall can still be found, however, the most obvious being the imposing gates at Rudolfplatz (Hahnentor), Ebertplatz to the north (Eigelsteintor) and Chlodwigplatz to the south (Severinstor), which are all easily accessible.

Traffic dominates the tree-fringed ring road itself during the day and although it's lined with bars, restaurants and cinemas, there is little to keep the visitor here before nightfall. But during the relative peace and quiet of the day it's worth ducking off the ring road to explore the smaller and more interesting streets around it. Heading back towards the centre, the area between Friesenstrasse and Mittelstrasse contains a maze of trendy shopping streets, where

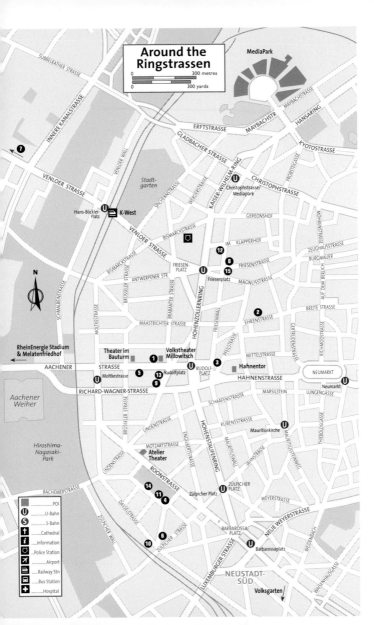

Around the Ringstrassen

0	300 metres
0	300 yards

MediaPark

SUBBELRATHER STRASSE

INNERE KANALSTRASSE

VENLOER STRASSE

ERFTSTRASSE

MAYBACHSTR

HANSARING

KYOTOSTRASSE

GLADBACHER STRASSE

KAISER-WILHELM-RING

CHRISTOPHSTRASSE

Christophstrasse/
Mediapark

Stadt-
garten

VENLOER STRASSE

Hans-Böckler-
Platz

K-West

BISMARCKSTRASSE

GEREONSHOF

ZEUGHAUSSTRASSE

BURGMAUER

AUF DEM BERLICH

IM KLAPPERHOF

FRIESENSTRASSE

12

8

15

FRIESEN-
PLATZ

Friesenplatz

MAGNUSSTRASSE

BREITE STRASSE

ANTWERPENER STR

MAASTRICHTER STRASSE

BISMARCKSTRASSE

BRÜSSELER STRASSE

BRABANTER STRASSE

HOHENZOLLERNRING

FRIESENWALL

PFEILSTRASSE

2

EHRENSTRASSE

MITTELSTRASSE

GERTRUDENSTRASSE

SCHWALBENGASSE

MOLTKESTRASSE

Theater im
Bauturm

Volkstheater
Millowitsch

1

3

Hahnentor

RUDOLF-
PLATZ

NEUMARKT

Neumarkt

LUNGENGASSE

AACHENER

STRASSE

Moltkestrasse

5

13

9

HAHNENSTRASSE

MARSILSTEIN

RheinEnergie Stadium
& Melatenfriedhof

RICHARD-WAGNER-STRASSE

SCHAAFENSTRASSE

LINDENSTRASSE

RUBENSSTRASSE

THEBÄERGASSE

MAURITIUSSTEINWEG

Aachener
Weiher

Hiroshima-
Nagasaki-
Park

BRÜSSELER STRASSE

ENGELBERTSTRASSE

HOHENSTAUFENRING

MAURITIUSWALL

Mauritiuskirche

MAURITIUSWALL

JAHNSTRASSE

MOTZARTSTRASSE

Atelier
Theater

ROONSTRASSE

ZÜLPICHER
PLATZ

BACHEMERSTRASSE

14

11

4

Zülpicher Platz

WEYERSTRASSE

LINDENSTRASSE

DASSELSTRASSE

ZÜLPICHER WALL

ZÜLPICHER STRASSE

6

10

BARBAROSSA
PLATZ

NEUE WEYERSTRASSE

WEIDENBACH

LUXEMBURGER STRASSE

Barbarossaplatz

NEUSTADT-
SÜD

Volksgarten

WAGENHAUSGASSE

N

▢	POI
Ⓤ	U-Bahn
Ⓢ	S-Bahn
✝	Cathedral
ⓘ	Information
✖	Police Station
✈	Airport
🚉	Railway Stn
🚌	Bus Station
✚	Hospital

7

> **STADTGARTEN (CITY PARK)**
> If the bustle of the city is getting too much for you then just
> a short walk away on Venloer Strasse is Cologne's oldest park,
> the Stadtgarten. Laid out in 1827–9, its tall mature trees and
> well-kept lawns create a peaceful green bubble, where locals
> go to walk, relax and sunbathe. More than that, it also has an
> excellent café-restaurant and beer garden and is home to –
> and shares its name with – one of the city's best-known
> music venues.

cool clothes and shoes, both new and second-hand, can be found
alongside cafés, restaurants and clubs. This district also has a historical
site, at the city-centre end of Friesenstrasse, in the form of the round,
castellated tower that stood on the northwestern corner of the
Roman city walls, which houses a well-preserved mosaic.

On the other side of the ring road, to the west of Friesenplatz
and Rudolfplatz, is the Belgian quarter, easily identified by the street
names. If you have time for a walk here, you'll soon discover the
attractive old buildings and expensive apartments that make it one
of the most fashionable places to live in the city. This area is also
home to some classier and inevitably more expensive bars and
restaurants, making it a good choice for a romantic meal.

CULTURE

Jazz and theatre are two of the city's passions and this area has its
fair share of music venues and theatres. Both modern and traditional
productions are frequently staged, and although most are in German

⬥ *Acres of space to unwind in the Stadtgarten*

they will undoubtedly provide some insight into the city's famous sense of humour.

Atelier Theater Cabaret and satire are the specialities here, sometimes accompanied by live music. The 99 seats tend to sell out fast and the programme usually changes weekly. Open until 01.00, the theatre's café-bar is a great place for a pre- and post-performance drink.
Ⓐ Roonstrasse 78 Ⓣ 0221-242 485 Ⓦ www.ateliertheater.de
Ⓛ Shows 20.30, Box office 18.00–20.00 Ⓝ Tram/U-bahn: Zülpicherplatz

Stadtgarten The venue at the Venloer Strasse side of the Stadtgarten shares its name with the park and has been a well-known jazz stronghold in the city since the 1970s. Today it remains one of the best places in Cologne to hear jazz, although it also plays host to all kinds of contemporary music. The on-site café-restaurant also holds monthly changing exhibitions of new German art.
Ⓐ Venloer Str. 40 Ⓣ 0221-952 9940 Ⓦ www.stadtgarten.de
Ⓝ U-bahn Hans-Bocklerplatz; Train: Köln-West

Theater im Bauturm Energetic and ambitious contemporary works are performed at this small, modern theatre. Ⓐ Aachener Str. 24
Ⓣ 0221-524 242 Ⓦ www.theater-im-bauturm.de Ⓛ Box office
17.00–20.00 Mon–Fri, closed Sat & Sun Ⓝ U-Bahn: Rudolfplatz

Volkstheater Millowitsch Something of a Cologne institution, this traditional theatre, with its plush red seats, is home to the city's favourite folk theatre. The Millowitsch family has performed here, in comedic tales of everyday life, for 200 years, and Peter, the seventh generation, is as enthusiastic as ever. His late father Willy took his acclaimed performances from the stage to the wider

🔺 *Memorial to the much-loved Willy Millowitsch*

TV audience and was considered to be the personification of everything *Kölsch*. 🅐 Aachener Str. 5 🅣 0221-251 747 🅦 www.millowitsch.de
🕒 Box office open three hours prior to performances
Ⓝ U-Bahn: Rudolfplatz

RETAIL THERAPY

Shopping in this part of town is more of an adventure than in the giant chain stores a 15-minute walk away. Quirky emporiums full of ethnic goods and cheap jewellery rub shoulders with slick stores selling skateboarding gear on the more affordable Ehrenstrasse, while exclusive boutiques line Mittelstrasse. Frequented by a young and disconcertingly good-looking crowd, these are the streets on which to see and be seen.

Apropos One of those shops that gives you plenty of warning you can't afford anything in it before you even get through the door. Turn off the street into a fuchsia tunnel, which leads into a covered leafy square with a chic café. From here you enter the shop itself, which is packed with collections from many designer names and has an enviable selection of jeans. ⓐ Mittelstr. 3 ⓦ www.apropos-coeln.de ⓛ 10.00–19.00 Mon–Sat, closed Sun ⓝ U-Bahn: Rudolfplatz

Carhartt Baggy skateboard gear for men and women. ⓐ Ehrenstr. 73 ⓦ www.carhartt.com ⓛ 11.00–20.00 Mon–Fri, 11.00–18.00 Sat, closed Sun ⓝ U-Bahn: Rudolfplatz or Friesenplatz

Diesel Jeans and casual wear for men and women. ⓐ Ehrenstr. 69 ⓛ 11.00–20.00 Mon–Sat, closed Sun ⓝ U-Bahn: Rudolfplatz

Doubleight Cool skater and surf clothing, plus helpful staff. ⓐ Ehrenstr. 65 ⓛ 12.00–20.00 Mon–Fri, 11.00–20.00 Sat, closed Sun ⓝ U-Bahn: Rudolfplatz or Friesenplatz

Hört Hört Everything percussion, including tambourines, bongos and steel drums. Not surprisingly, it can be noisy.

◎ Engelbert Str. 46 ⏱ 11.00–19.00 Mon–Fri, 11.00–16.00 Sat, closed Sun ◎ U-Bahn: Rudolfplatz

Invito Loud music, cool shoes, trainers and bags crammed into a small shop, which gets packed on Saturdays. ◎ Ehrenstr. 54a ☎ 0221-257 4686 ⏱ 10.00–20.00 Mon–Fri, 10.00–16.00 Sat, closed Sun ◎-U-Bahn: Rudolfplatz or Friesenplatz

Lapis Independent jewellers specialising in modern designs with lapis lazuli set in gold and silver. ◎ Friesenstr. 73–75 ☎ 0221-258 9798 ⏱ 10.30–13.30, 14.30–18.30 Mon–Fri, 10.30–16.00 Sat, closed Sun ◎-U-Bahn: Friesenplatz

Loft Trendy, warehouse-like clothes shop for men and women with a huge mirrored wall and bar at the back. ◎ Ehrenstr. 80–82 ⏱ 11.00–20.00 Mon–Fri, 11.00–16.00 Sat, closed Sun ◎-U-Bahn: Rudolfplatz or Friesenplatz

MAC Modern, bold cosmetics in a sleek white boutique. ◎ Ehrenstr. 44 ⏱ 11.00–19.30 Mon–Fri, 11.00–18.00 Sat, closed Sun ◎-U-Bahn: Rudolfplatz or Friesenplatz

Papelito An Aladdin's cave of beautiful stationery, paper models, decorations, books, photo albums and unique postcards. ◎ Zülpicherstr. 22 ☎ 0221-240 9786 ⏱ 11.00–19.00 Mon–Fri, 11.00–16.00 Sat, closed Sun ◎ U-Bahn: Zülpicherplatz

Tausend Fliegende Fische Popular new and used clothes shop, with some wild designs that aren't always cheap. Huge mirror and velvet-curtained changing rooms make trying on all the more tempting. ⓐ Roonstr. 18 ⓣ 0221-240 0233 ⓛ 11.00–20.00 Mon–Fri, 11.00–16.00 Sat, closed Sun ⓝ U-Bahn: Barbarossaplatz

TAKING A BREAK

There are so many enticing and eccentrically themed cafés, ice cream parlours and bars in this part of town that the chances are that sightseeing will provide a break from them rather than the other way round. That's no bad thing, and the locals, especially the students, seem to find as much time to spend sipping their drinks and chatting with friends as the tourists do.

Café Bauturm £ ❶ Eclectic interior with book pages papering the ceiling and chandeliers made from broken bottles. Frequented by artistic types and serving coffee, alcohol and good food from early until late. ⓐ Aachnerstr. 24 ⓣ 0221-528 984 ⓛ 08.00–03.00 Mon–Fri, 09.00–03.00 Sat & Sun ⓝ U-Bahn: Rudolfplatz

Café Waschsalon £ ❷ Full of launderette chic, with washing machine drums serving as light shades. Drinks, snacks and light meals all day. ⓐ Ehrenstr. 77 ⓣ 0221-133 378 ⓛ 10.00–01.00 Mon–Thur, 10.00–03.00 Fri & Sat, 14.00–01.00 Sun ⓝ-U-Bahn: Rudolfplatz or Friesenplatz

Eis Café Breda £ ❸ Sit out on Rudolfplatz on a sunny day and enjoy indulgent ice creams, coffees and snacks. ⓐ Pfeilstr. 2–4 ⓣ 0221-257 3164 ⓝ-U-Bahn: Rudolfplatz

Feysinn £ ❹ Slightly studenty bar-bistro, with an attractive mirrored bar, street seating and cheap, tasty lunches. ⓐ Rathenaupl. 7 ⓣ 0221-

240 9210 🕐 09.00–01.00 Mon–Thur, 09.00–02.00 Fri, 09.30–02.00 Sat, 10.00–01.00 Sun Ⓝ U-Bahn: Dasselstrasse; Train: Köln-Süd

Kaffee Storch £ ❺ Relaxed café that often plays old jazz tracks. It's a popular hang-out – Mondays from 23.30 feature open-mike poetry readings, while from the same time on Tuesdays anyone can show off their latest video artwork. ⓐ Aachener Str. 17 ☏ 0221-251 717 🕐 09.00–01.00 Ⓝ U-Bahn: Rudolfplatz

Magnus £ ❻ A big café-bar with a brightly painted interior, varied menu and generous portions. Come here for cocktails in the evening. ⓐ Zülpicherstr. 48 ☏ 0221-241 469 ⓦ www.cafemagnus.de 🕐 09.00–02.00 Mon–Fri, 09.00–03.00 Sat & Sun Ⓝ U-Bahn: Zülpicherplatz

AFTER DARK

The area around the ring road really comes to life in the evening, with a huge range of excellent bars, restaurants and clubs frequented by locals every night of the week. On the ring road itself are the big bar-restaurants, many with live music or their own party atmosphere, which are a good place to start before hitting the clubs, none of which open before 22.00. In the smaller streets between Rudolfplatz and Friesenplatz you'll find more intimate restaurants and fashionable cocktail bars that often stay open until 05.00 at the weekend. There's no reason to ignore the student area, either: centred on Zülpicherstrasse, it is filled with lively bars, and good, reasonably priced restaurants. The ultra-stylish Rathenauplatz nearby is home to romantic restaurants, which are popular with the city's Porsche-driving set, as well as a busy park with a beer garden and children's playground.

RESTAURANTS

Selam £ ❼ Not much to look at from the outside, this Ethiopian restaurant serves a range of extremely tasty but cheap dishes eaten the traditional way, with Injera bread instead of cutlery.
ⓐ Ehrenfeldgürtel 91 ❶ 0221-952 0352 ⓦ www.selam-restaurant.de
❶ 15.00–01.00 Mon–Fri, 13.00–01.00 Sat & Sun ⓝ U-Bahn: Venloer Strasse

Sushi Nara 2 £ ❽ The best kind of sushi bar, with a central conveyor belt surrounded by high stools. Also serves noodle dishes. Reasonable prices. ⓐ Friesenstr. 57 ❶ 0221-120 170 ❶ 12.00–15.00, 17.30–23.00 Mon–Sat, 17.00–22.00 Sun ⓝ U-Bahn: Friesenplatz

Türkiye Pazari £ ❾ An informal diner that's always packed with people enjoying kebabs and Turkish specialities from the hotplate that's visible through the window. ⓐ Händelstr. 51 ❶ 0221-252 674
ⓝ U-Bahn: Rudolfplatz

Zarathustra £ ❿ Popular Persian restaurant with incredibly fragrant kebab and meat dishes cooked in a traditional oven. Also does take-away. ⓐ Dasselstr. 4 ❶ 0221-240 7660 ❶ 12.00–24.00 ⓝ U-Bahn: Dasselstrasse; Train: Köln-Süd

Chichos £–££ ⓫ For a party atmosphere, try this Latin American restaurant, where top-quality food, cheap cocktails and the occasional musical interlude guarantee a good time. ⓐ Rathenaupl. 1
❶ 0221-240 5656 ❶ 17.30–24.00 Sun–Thur, 17.30–01.00 Fri & Sat
ⓝ U-Bahn: Dasselstrasse; Train: Köln-Süd

Maru £–££ ⓬ This Asian fusion restaurant and bar is a great place for dim sum, which is otherwise hard to find in Germany.

Good vegetarian options, too. ⓐ Hildeboldpl. 1a ⓣ 0221-200 5543
ⓦ www.marucafe.org ⓛ 12.00–15.00, 17.30–23.00 Tues–Fri,
15.00–24.00 Sat, 15.00–02.00 Sun ⓝ U-Bahn: Friesenplatz

Tandoor Palace £–££ ⓭ A classy Indian restaurant with a crisp clean
interior and walls decorated with painted flowers. Friendly, family-run
place producing consistently good food. ⓐ Händelstr. 33 ⓣ 0221-236855
ⓦ www.tandoorpalace.de ⓛ 12.00–14.30, 18.00–23.30 Sun–Fri,
18.00–23.30 Sat ⓝ U-Bahn: Rudolfplatz

Weinstube Bacchus ££ ⓮ Busy and friendly, this excellent bistro has
a cosy wood-panelled interior, a well-chosen wine list and perfectly
cooked meat and fish dishes. ⓐ Rathenaupl. 17 ⓣ 0221-217 986
ⓛ 17.00–01.00 Mon–Fri, 18.00–01.00 Sat & Sun ⓝ U-Bahn:
Dasselstrasse; Train: Köln-Süd

🔺 *It's a moveable feast*

Heising & Adelmann £££ ⓯ Cologne's in-crowd flock to this stylish (if pricey) bar-restaurant for its meat- and fish-based menu, which is more creative than many others in the city. ⓐ Friesenstr. 58–60 ⓣ 0221-130 9424 ⓦ www.heising-und-adelmann.de ⓛ 18.00–03.00 Mon–Sat, closed Sun ⓝ U-Bahn: Friesenplatz

BARS & CLUBS

Breugel Brasserie Cocktail bar and restaurant with a moody, dark interior and grand piano. Musicians perform every night and there's outdoor seating in summer. ⓐ Hohenzollering 17 ⓣ 0221-252 579 ⓦ www.bruegel.de ⓛ 12.00–03.00 Mon–Fri, 18.00–03.00 Sat & Sun ⓝ U-Bahn: Rudolfplatz

Diamond Club Classy white interior and cool lighting make this the ideal destination for fans of house music. ⓐ Hohenzollering 90 ⓦ www.club-diamond.de ⓛ 22.00–05.00 ⓝ U-Bahn: Friesenplatz. Admission charge

Hallmackenreuther Two-storey bar with DJs and chic 1960's decor. It's popular with students during the day, while at night it attracts a well-groomed thirtysomething crowd, most of whom work in media or design. ⓐ Brüsseler Platz 9 ⓣ 0221-517 970 ⓛ Bar 11.00–01.00 ⓝ U-Bahn: Moltkestrasse

Jameson's Irish Pub Huge Irish theme bar, with sports events shown on two big screens, and live music on Thursday and Friday. ⓐ Friesenstr. 30–40 ⓣ 0221-912 3323 ⓦ www.jamesonpubs.com ⓛ 12.00–01.00 Mon–Thur, 12.00–03.00 Fri & Sat, 11.00–01.00 Sun ⓝ U-Bahn: Friesenplatz

Päff This place could be described as a dive, with a laid-back atmosphere and equally relaxed clientele. For the (slightly) more energetic there's a dance floor in the basement. ⓐ Friesenwall 130 ☎ 0221-121 060 🌐 www.paeff.com 🕒 20.00–02.00 Sun–Thur, 20.00–03.00 Fri & Sat Ⓝ U-Bahn: Friesenplatz

Scheinbar Retro-style bar replete with lava lamps and low lighting. The mixed relaxed crowd enjoys funk, electro and anything in between. The cosy corner tables fill up quickly, so arrive early. ⓐ Brüsselerstr. 10 ☎ 0221-923 2048 🕒 20.00–03.00 Mon–Thur, 20.00–05.00 Fri & Sat, closed Sun Ⓝ U-Bahn: Moltkestrasse

Triple A Ranked among Germany's top clubs, with different DJs every night of the week, playing everything from chart sounds and techno to soul and classic disco. ⓐ An d'r Hahnepooz 8 (Rudolfplatz) 🌐 www.triplea-club.de 🕒 23.00–late Ⓝ U-Bahn: Rudolfplatz. Admission charge

Umbruch Small, atmospheric bar with seats at the front and a dance floor at the back. Plays hip-hop, funk, techno and house and is popular with the local students. ⓐ Zülpicherstr. 11 ☎ 0221-240 6622 🕒 20.00– 02.00 Sun–Thur, 20.00–03.00 Fri & Sat Ⓝ U-Bahn: Zülpicherstrasse

CINEMAS
Off Broadway Set back from the street through an archway, this small art-house cinema shows films (including British and American) in their original version, subtitled in German. ⓐ Zülpicherstr. 24 ☎ 0221-232 418 🌐 www.off-broadway.de Ⓝ U-Bahn: Zülpicherstrasse

Outside the centre

As you move away from the city centre, Cologne rapidly gets greener, as it's almost completely encircled by well-kept, well-used parks. Other attractions, such as the zoo, Rhine cable car and MediaPark, are easy to reach by public transport and will occupy adults and kids alike for hours. However, places to stop for lunch and a snack are not as forthcoming as they are in the centre, so if you're planning a day in the park, a picnic would be the perfect solution. Remember to pack your swimming kit, too, as there are great pools and thermal baths where you can either splash around or relax and unwind.

SIGHTS & ATTRACTIONS

Many of these attractions could happily take up a whole day if you let them. Some, especially the zoo, swimming pool and Rheinpark, can get busy at weekends, when local families swell the tourist numbers. Don't let that put you off, though: it just adds to the atmosphere.

Claudius Therme (Thermal baths)
To take relaxation to another level, try this luxurious spa, located in the Rheinpark close to the cable car. A natural thermal mineral spring provides the complex's numerous indoor and outdoor pools with therapeutic water, which you can soak and swim in. There are solariums, saunas and steam baths, and you can also hire towels and swimming costumes. Day tickets to use all the facilities are quite expensive, but you will probably want to stay that long. Massages and beauty treatments are available for an extra charge, although they need to be pre-booked. ❸ Sachsenburgstr. 1

1 0221-981 440 **W** www.claudius-therme.de **L** 09.00–24.00
N Bus: 150; U-Bahn: Zoo/Flora then cable car. Admission charge

Eis- & Schwimmstadion

A short walk from the zoo is this excellent leisure complex, with
outdoor pools open from May to the beginning of September, as well
as a climbing wall and basketball courts. In winter there's an ice rink.
a Lentstr. 30 **1** 0221-726 026 **L** 10.00–20.00 Mon–Fri, 09.00–20.00 Sat
& Sun **N** U-Bahn: Zoo/Flora. Admission charge

Flora & Botanischer Garten (Botanic Garden)

Head through the archway past the zoo ticket office and cross the
road to reach the magnificent wrought-iron gates at the entrance to
this garden. Once you are through them stop to admire the brightly
planted parterre, sparkling fountain and the grand Flora building
beyond. This 19th-century park is a beautiful, colourful place to take
a stroll on a sunny day. A network of paths runs between the mature
trees, past statues and sculptures, to the small, natural-looking lake
featuring a statue of Neptune and terrapins. There are also several
glasshouses, with an amazing selection of cacti. *Die Flora* café (see
page 116) in the central building serves light lunch, ice creams and
cold drinks – at a price. **a** Amsterdamer Str. 34 **1** 0221-560 890
L 08.00–21.00 (summer), 08.00–dusk (winter) **N** U-Bahn: Zoo/Flora

Hansa-Hochhaus (Hansa skyscraper)

Just a stone's throw from the MediaPark is another of Cologne's
highest buildings. The slightly forbidding Hansa-Hochhaus was
Europe's tallest skyscraper in the 1920s, reaching a height of 65 m
(200 ft), although that looks diminutive by today's standards. It now
houses the huge Saturn music store over several of its floors, which

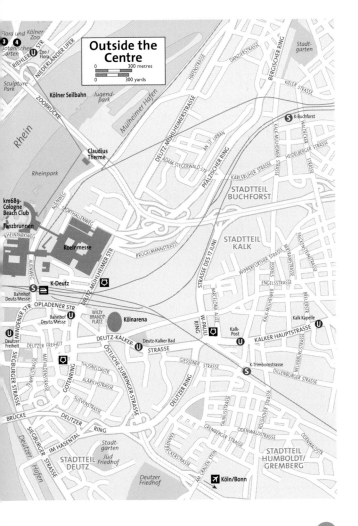

stocks CDs in every genre. Warning: once you start listening to sample tracks on the headphones, it's hard to stop. **Saturn** ⓐ Am Hansaring ❶ 0221-161 6260 ❷ 10.00–20.00 Mon–Sat, closed Sun Ⓦ U-Bahn: Hansaring

km689 – Cologne Beach Club

If you prefer to lie on sand rather than grass, then stop by Rheinpark's lively beach venue, whose entrance is opposite the café. A huge area of safe, clean sand runs down to the riverbank and there are hammocks and deckchairs as well as DJs and bars serving cocktails and snacks. When the sun is out this place is very popular, so get there early to bag the best spot. ⓐ Rheinterrassen 1 Ⓦ www.km689.rhein-terrassen.de ❷ 12.00–01.00 May–Sept Ⓦ Bus: 150 to Tanzbrunnen. Admission charge

Kölnarena

This impressive stadium, with its glass façade spanned by a 76 m (250 ft) high steel arc, is known locally as the 'lunch basket'. It uses its full potential to host huge pop concerts and stage shows with audiences of up to 19,000. It's also home to the city's ice hockey, basketball and handball teams and serves as a venue for prestigious sporting events, such as the Ice Hockey World Championship in 2001. ⓐ Willy Brandt Pl. 1 ❶ 0221–8020 for tickets Ⓦ www.koelnarena.de Ⓦ Tram/Bus: Bahnhof Deutz/Messe, Köln-Deutz or Deutz-Kalker Bad

Kölner Zoo (Cologne Zoo)

Extremely popular with animal lovers of all ages, this zoo keeps more than 500 species in total, representing every continent and ocean. The enormous *Elefantenpark* is a highlight, as it allows the

---

❷ *The basket-shaped Kölnarena doubles as a stadium and a concert venue*

elephants space to behave and interact more as they might in the wild. It's also fascinating to watch the group of 150 baboons on their own island, doing what baboons do. There are also great apes, reptiles and insects, as well as a huge aquarium and steamy Southeast Asian jungle, complete with free-flying birds. Feeding times for the different animals are posted near the entrance, and if you're hungry yourself there are snack bars, a café and a restaurant where you can refuel. Outside the zoo, between the ticket office and U-Bahn station, there are also good pretzel stands and a kiosk selling sweets and drinks.
ⓐ Riehler Str. 173 ⓣ 0221-77850 ⓦ www.zoo-koeln.de ⓛ 09.00–18.00 (summer), 09.00–17.00 (winter) ⓝ U-Bahn: Zoo/Flora. Admission charge

⬤ *If you've got a head for heights the cable car is a great way to see Cologne*

KÖLNER SEILBAHN (CABLE CAR)

By far the most scenic way to cross the Rhine, the cable car runs from opposite the zoo, high above the river, over to the Rheinpark. From this vantage point you get a brilliant view back over the Cologne skyline, where the cathedral towers soar above everything else. If you're afraid of heights and have second thoughts, note that there's a walkway across the bridge below, which gives easy access to the Rheinpark.
ⓐ Riehler Str. 180 ⓣ 0221-547 4184 ⓦ www.koelner-seilbahn.de
ⓛ 10.00–18.00 late Mar–early Nov, closed early Nov–late Mar
Ⓤ U-Bahn: Zoo/Flora. Admission charge

MediaPark

For a taste of modern Cologne, visit the newly developed MediaPark in the north of the city, just outside the ring road. This former freight depot is now covered with sleek offices, which house TV and radio stations and media giants like EMI and Sony Music. A new landmark is the rather beautiful **KölnTurm**, a tapering glass skyscraper that is reflected in the park's lake. There are many restaurants and shops here, as well as the *Cinedom*, Cologne's biggest and busiest cinema, with a terrace café on its roof that boasts good views. ⓦ www.mediapark.de
Ⓤ U-Bahn: Christophstrasse/MediaPark

Melatenfriedhof (Melaten Cemetery)

This huge public cemetery, which is more like a park than a burial ground, lies just three tram stops from Rudolfsplatz. The old trees, grassy meadows and elaborate gravestones make it a perfect resting place for the living as well as the dead. Melaten was built in the early

1800s after Napoleon ordered that all burials should take place outside the city, in accordance with the traditions of ancient Rome. The name comes from the French *malade* (sick), and is a reference to the disused lepers' colony that the cemetery was built on.
ⓐ Aachener Str. Ⓦ www.melatenfriedhof.de Ⓛ 07.00–20.00 Apr–Oct, 08.00–17.00 Nov–Mar Ⓝ U-bahn: Melaten

RheinEnergie Stadium

Home to the *Bundesliga* team FC Köln, who play in red and white, the former Müngersdorfer stadium, built in 1975, was transformed into a state-of-the-art venue for the 2006 FIFA World Cup. The stadium also hosts pop concerts from time to time. Guided tours take place on weekday evenings. ⓐ Aachener Str. 999 Ⓣ 0221-498 3806 Ⓦ www.stadion-koeln.de Ⓛ Tours 17.00–19.00 Mon–Fri (excluding match days), closed Sat & Sun. FC Köln match tickets available from Ⓣ 01805 325 656 or Ⓦ www.fc-tickets.de Ⓝ Tram: RheinEnergie-Stadion. Admission charge

Rheinpark

At about 50 hectares (125 acres), this is Cologne's largest park and is so big that there's a miniature railway to carry you from one end to the other, although cycling and rollerblading are popular alternatives. Local families flock here on sunny days, especially Sundays, for picnics, barbecues, football, fun on the big adventure playground and general relaxation. There are also great views along the Rhine back to the city, and the cathedral towers are always visible through the treetops. At the opposite end of the park from the cable car is a café selling drinks and snacks. The nearby stage, surrounded by a famous dancing fountain (Tanzbrunnen), hosts concerts in the evening (see page 115). Ⓝ U-Bahn: Zoo/flora then cable car; train: S6, 11 or 12

⬤ The RheinEnergie Stadium is home to the city's football heroes

Volksgarten (People's Park)

In the south of the city, another of the city's great parks, Volksgarten, is notable for its large, tranquil lake. Pedalos and rowing boats are available for hire, so the water is never still for long. Among the well-kept grass and mature trees is a beer garden, which has been in the same spot since 1891 and serves excellent *Kölsch* and snacks. Ⓝ Tram: Eifelplatz

CULTURE

As you get into the fringes of Cologne, the art and culture of the centre begins to dry up. If you're passing, the Sculpture Park is worth a visit, if only to put your art critic hat on for a while, or you could keep your eye out for it as you glide over in the cable car. The Tanzbrunnen concerts aren't regular, so check listings for details.

Kölner Karnevalsmuseum (Cologne Carnival Museum)

This museum details the history of the traditional festival from Roman times to the present day. The documents showing minutes from historical carnival club meetings probably aren't that exciting for non-Kölners, but the costumes, and music and videos give a good idea of the event for those who aren't lucky enough to see the real thing. ❸ Maarweg 134–136 ❶ 0221-574 0076 Ⓦ www.kk-museum.de ❶ 10.00–20.00 Thur, 10.00–17.00 Fri, 11.00–17.00 Sat & Sun, open for groups Tues, Wed on request, closed Mon & during carnival Ⓝ Tram: Maarweg; bus: 141, 143 to Widdersdorfer Strasse/Maarweg. Admission charge

Sculpture Park

Close to the zoo, this green space on the banks of the Rhine is scattered with a permanent exhibition of 30 works of modern sculpture. The park was opened in 1997 as part of the Art Cologne festival and has been the subject of much debate ever since. Pieces by artists such as Cragg, Förg and Suvero number among the collection, so why not go and judge for yourself? ❷ Access via Riehler Str., next to the Zoobrücke (bridge) ◷ 10.30–18.30 Mar, Apr, Sept & Oct; 10.30–19.00 May–Aug; 10.30–16.30 Nov–Feb ◎ U-Bahn: Zoo/Flora

Tanzbrunnen

Clustered at the opposite end of the Rheinpark from the cable car is a range of venues hosting various kinds of entertainment throughout the year. The one to look out for is the circular stage that shelters under a winged, tent-like structure and is surrounded by water. The fountains in the pool are illuminated while they perform their own dance during the classical and pop concerts that take place on the stage. There's another, larger, outdoor stage and a big indoor venue where music and comedy are performed and clubbing nights keep the party going into the early hours. Listings magazines and ticket offices have programme details. ⓐ Rheinparkweg 1 ❶ 0221-821 3183 Tickets available from Köln Tickets ❶ 0221-2801 ⓦ www.koelnticket.de ◎ Train/Tram: Köln-Deutz

TAKING A BREAK

If the weather's nice, pack a picnic. Otherwise, there's a selection of places to get a drink or have lunch, as well as the catering facilities in the zoo. Many of the bars and restaurants listed below in the After Dark section also serve food and drinks during the day.

Biergarten Volksgarten £ ❶ A leafy spot to drink beer, lunch on

pizza and salad and indulge in home-made cakes in the afternoon. ⓐ Volksgartenstr. 27 ❶ 0221-382 626 ◷ 11.30–01.00 ◎ U-Bahn: Eifelplatz

La Gelateria – Eiscafé Paradiso £ ❷ Italian-style ice creams, coffee and snacks, with a panoramic view of the MediaPark from the roof of the Cinedom. ❸ Im MediaPark 1 ❶ 0221-9519 5226 ◷ 14.00–24.00 Mon–Fri, 12.00–24.00 Sat & Sun Ⓝ U-Bahn: Christophstrasse/MediaPark

Die Flora £–££ ❸ Pleasant terrace café in the Flora building, which serves good sandwiches, salads and hot meals as well as coffee and ice cream. ❶ 0221-763 046 ◷ 12.00–18.00 Ⓝ U-Bahn: Zoo/Flora

Garten Restaurant am Zoo-Eck £–££ ❹ Conveniently nestled between the zoo and the botanic garden, this is the place for steaks, big mixed grills and salads. ❶ 0221-765 391 ◷ 11.30–23.00 Ⓝ U-Bahn: Zoo/Flora

AFTER DARK

There is still plenty of nightlife outside the city centre, and one of the best places to be in summer is sipping a drink on Köln beach watching the sun set over the old town. Indeed, walking along the Deutz bank of the Rhine at night gives some great views over to the illuminated cathedral. There are also lively bars and restaurants in the MediaPark, in the north of the city (Nordstadt) near Ebertplatz, and in the south (Südstadt) near Chlodwigplatz.

RESTAURANTS

Engelbät £ ❺ This Südstadt crêperie is a great place for pancakes or just a beer and a chat. Live jazz accompanies either brunch or dinner on Sundays. ❸ Engelbertstr. 7 ❶ 0221-246 914 Ⓦ www.engelbaet.de ◷ 11.00–01.00 Ⓝ U-Bahn: Barbarossaplatz

Ocean Drive £–££ ❻ American-style diner in the Cinedom complex, complete with neon lights. Menu of burgers, steaks, ribs and salads, as well as draught beer and cocktails. ❸ In Cinedom, MediaPark 1 ❶ 0221-9519 5304 ❹ 17.00–24.00 Ⓝ U-Bahn: Christophstrasse/MediaPark

La Patata ££ ❼ Tiny, almost cramped, traditional family-run Spanish restaurant in Südstadt, serving some of the best tapas in town. Worth a visit. ❸ Kurfürstenstr. 24 ❶ 0221-31692 ❹ 18.00–24.00 Ⓝ U-Bahn: Chlodwigplatz

Pantanal Rodizio ££ ❽ Make sure you're hungry before coming to this Nordstadt restaurant because waiters will keep bringing the delicious Brazilian *rodizio* salad buffet and meat kebabs until you tell them to stop. ❸ Maybachstr. 22 ❶ 0221-130 1767 ❹ 18.00–24.00 Mon–Sat, 12.00–24.00 Sun Ⓝ U-Bahn: Christophstrasse/MediaPark

Osman 30 ££–£££ ❾ This chic top-scale restaurant on the 30th floor of the MediaPark has an amazing view over Cologne's skyscrapers and cathedral. The food is excellent and the wine list extensive. Great on sunny Sundays, when brunch is served on the enormous terrace. ❸ Im Mediapark 8 ❶ 0221-5005 2080 Ⓦ www.osman-cologne.de ❹ 18.00–01.00 Mon–Thur, 18.00–03.00 Fri & Sat, 11.00–18.30 Sun Ⓝ U-Bahn: Christophstrasse/MediaPark

BARS
Elektra Despite appearances, this dark and moody retro bar in the Nordstadt is very friendly, with good DJs and a recommended Sunday brunch. ❸ Gereonswall 12–14 Ⓦ www.elektrabar.de ❹ 12.00–01.00 Ⓝ U-Bahn: Hansaring

Fiffi Bar A completely mad, dog-themed bar on a corner not far from the Volksgarten. Even the cocktails have canine-related names. Rolandstr. 99 0221-340 6211 www.fiffibar.de 21.00–02.00 Sun–Thur, 21.00–03.00 Fri & Sat U-Bahn: Chlodwigplatz

Spitz This lovely, cosy café-bar, with a long wooden bar and high stools, is in the Nordstadt. Crisply dressed waiters bring good coffee, beer, cakes and meals. Lübeckerstr. 1 0221-131 625 09.00–01.00 Mon–Fri, 09.00–02.00 Sat, 10.00–01.00 Sun U-Bahn: Ebertplatz

Underground If you're into heavy metal, rock and punk, then this historic club is for you. Pub, concert rooms and beer garden in a former warehouse. Vogelsangerstr. 200 Information 0221-542 326, Tickets 0221-954 2990 www.underground-cologne.de 18.00–late U-bahn: Venloer Strasse/Gürtel

CINEMAS

Cinedom Cologne's largest and busiest cinema has 14 screens and regularly hosts film premieres. For some visitors the gloss will be lost as movies are screened in German. Im MediaPark 1 0221-9519 5195 www.cinedom.de U-Bahn: Christophstrasse/MediaPark

Metropolis The best English-language cinema option in the city, this venue shows current films in their original form, often not even subtitled. Ebertpl. 19 Pre-recorded information on screening times 0221-739 245 (wait for the English version after the German), Tickets 0221-722 436 www.metropolis-koeln.de U-Bahn: Ebertplatz

---

Schloss Augustusburg in Brühl

Bonn

Just 30 km (19 miles) south of Cologne on the banks of the Rhine is Bonn, the perfect destination for a fascinating day trip. The capital of the Federal Republic of Germany between 1949 and 1991, Bonn is an energetic place filled with beautiful buildings, museums and art galleries, as well as great shops and colourful festivals. As it was the birthplace of Beethoven, classical music is also at the cultural heart of the city.

GETTING THERE

By rail

Transport links between Cologne and Bonn are excellent and depending on the type of train, the trip takes between 20 minutes and half hour from Cologne's main railway station. You can also hop

on the train to Bonn from Köln-West (Venloer Str.) and Köln-Süd (Luxemburger Str.) stations. For a cheaper but longer ride, a southbound tram on line 18 will take you to Bonn in an hour (for a one-way trip to Bonn, you will need to buy a City Plus 2b ticket).

By road

A hassle-free drive down the A555 Autobahn takes around 40 minutes, although for the visitor, parking and navigating Bonn's one-way streets can be a challenge.

By boat

A leisurely way to reach Bonn and see the lovely landscapes along the Rhine is to take a tour boat from Cologne. Depending on which boat you take, the trip can take between two and three and a half

On a sunny day, it can be difficult to find a free table at Bonn's Marktplatz

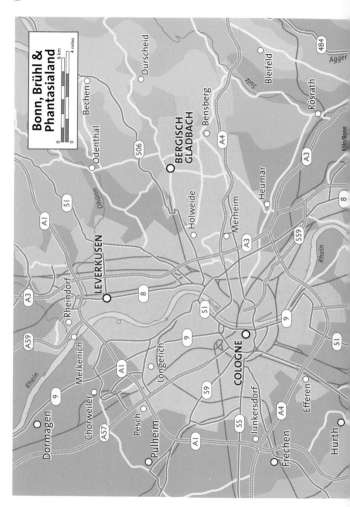

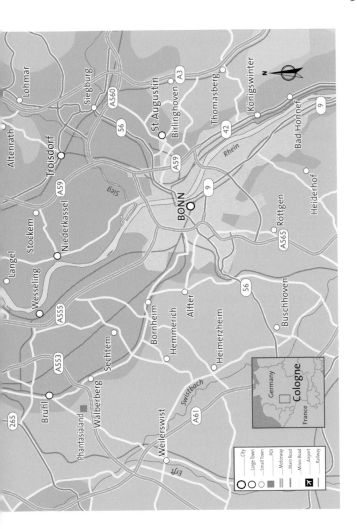

hours, so a one-way boat ticket and a train ride back will save time if necessary. Most cruises leave in the morning, so it can be worth checking times the day before. The company, Köln Düsseldorfer leaves from near the Fischmarkt on the Rhine (ⓐ Frankenwerft 35 ⓣ 0221-208 8318 ⓦ www.k-d.com), whereas Bonner Personen Schifffahrt (ⓣ 0228-636 363 ⓦ www.b-p-s.de) departs from under the Hohenzollernbrücke, just behind the Dom.

SIGHTS & ATTRACTIONS

Visitors who travel by train will arrive at the main station in the centre of Bonn's old town, and many of the top sights are only a short walk away. The tourist information office five minutes' walk from the station has useful maps and guides.
ⓐ Windeckstr. 1 on Münsterplatz ⓣ 0228-775 000

Altes Rathaus (Old Town Hall)
The marketplace is dominated by this imposing baroque building, completed in 1738 and visited by many dignitaries over the centuries. Numerous speeches have been given from the steps out front, including a welcome from President John F Kennedy in 1963.
ⓣ 0228-774 288 ⓛ 12.00–17.00 first Sat of month, May–Oct, closed Nov–Apr

Beethoven-Denkmal (Beethoven statue)
Bonn's favourite son is immortalised in bronze on Münsterplatz. The statue was unveiled in 1845 to commemorate the composer's 75th birthday (18 years after his death) and stands in front of the magnificent central post-office building, which was once a royal palace. (For the Beethoven Museum, see page 127.)

Marktplatz (Market Square)

A short walk along Remigiusstrasse brings you to Bonn's triangular market square, which still hosts thriving fruit and vegetable stalls, alongside cafés, shops and restaurants, making it an interesting place to linger and watch the world go by.

Münsterbasilika

The unmistakable spires of Bonn's biggest church are the first landmark to head for. Built between the 11th and 13th centuries on the graves of the city's patrons Cassius and Florentius, the basilica is a combination of Romanesque and Gothic architectural styles. Like so many buildings along the Rhine, it was damaged by World War II bombs, but has been fully restored. ⓐ Münsterpl. ⓣ 0228-985 880 ⓦ www.bonner-muenster.de ⓛ 07.00–19.00

POPPELSDORF DISTRICT

Heading away from Münsterplatz as you leave the main railway station will take you down the grand, tree-lined Poppelsdorfer Allee towards the spectacular Poppelsdorf Palace. This is a fashionable residential area with some beautiful art nouveau houses built in the 1870s, plus plenty of good cafés and restaurants.

Botanische Gärten (Botanical Gardens)

Formerly the castle gardens, this six-hectare (15-acre) plot was assigned to the university in 1818 and today is filled with interesting plants and tropical greenhouses – and people relaxing. ⓐ Meckheimer Allee 171 ⓣ 0228-735 523 ⓦ www.botgart.uni-bonn.de ⓛ 09.00–18.00 Mon–Fri & Sun, closed Sat, Apr–Oct; 09.00–16.00 Mon–Fri, 09.00–18.00 Sun, closed Sat, Nov–Mar. Conservatories open 10.00–12.00, 14.00–16.00 Mon–Fri, 09.00–18.00 Sun, closed Sat

Freizeitpark Rheinaue (Rheinaue Leisure Park)

This vast 160-hectare (395-acre) park, which straddles the river south of the old town, is home to sports facilities, playgrounds, barbecue areas and the 15-hectare (37-acre) meadow lake, at the north end of which pedalos and rowing boats can be hired. It's ideal for walking, sunbathing, picnicking or just watching the rollerbladers and model-boat fanatics.

The park also hosts the giant **Rheinkultur** music festival (first weekend in July), where huge crowds gather for free rock, pop, hip-hop and jazz concerts from well-known and local groups. ⓦ www.rheinkultur.com

Another crowd-pleaser is **Bonner Bierbörse (Bonn Beer Festival)** at the end of July, when more than 90 exhibitors provide a selection of international beers, along with open-air entertainment. ⓦ www.bierboerse.com

Poppelsdorfer Schloss (Poppelsdorf Palace)

Completed in 1753, this rococo pleasure palace is more reminiscent of a French château than a castle, but is impressive nonetheless. In 1818 it was assigned to house scientific collections from Bonn University and as such is now home to the rock and crystal collection of its mineralogical museum. ⓐ Meckenheimer Allee 171 ⓣ 0228-732 761 ⓛ Mineralogical Museum 15.00–17.00 Wed, 10.00–12.00 Sun, closed Mon, Tues & Thur–Sat

CULTURE

Arithmeum

Science and technology museum focusing on the history of counting, with the world's largest collection of historical mechanical calculating

SPOILT FOR CHOICE
There are so many museums, art galleries and music venues in Bonn that if you're only here for a short time the biggest problem will be deciding what to see. If you're planning on visiting several museums, you might want to invest in a Bonn Regio WelcomeCard (available from the tourist office), which provides free and reduced admission to some museums and galleries.

machines. It also features contemporary art inspired by geometrical patterns. Great for scientifically minded kids and adults. ⓐ Lennéstr. 2 ⓣ 0228-738 790 ⓦ www.arithmeum.uni-bonn.de ⓛ 11.00–18.00 Tues–Sun

Beethoven-Haus

An exhibition of the great composer's manuscripts, musical instruments and possessions, along with a tour of the house he was born in, give an insight into Beethoven's life and work. The attached Chamber Music Hall hosts concerts weekly in summer (see the website for details). ⓐ Bonngasse 18–26 ⓣ 0228-981 7525 ⓦ www.beethoven-haus-bonn.de ⓛ 10.00–18.00 Mon–Sat, 11.00–18.00 Sun, Apr–Oct; 10.00–17.00 Mon–Sat, 11.00–17.00 Sun, Nov–Mar ⓝ Tram: 62, 66 to Bertha-v-Suttner Pl. Admission charge

Deutsches Museum Bonn (German Museum)

If you like the monorail in front of the entrance, you'll spend hours in this museum of science and technology discovering the details behind everything from ship-building to space travel. ⓐ Ahrstr. 45 ⓣ 0228-302 252 ⓦ www.deutsches-museum.de ⓛ 10.00–18.00 Tues–Sun, closed Mon ⓝ U-Bahn/Tram: 16, 63; bus: 610, 614

Kunstmuseum Bonn (Art Museum)

The arresting contemporary building that is home to Bonn's modern art museum was designed by Axel Schultes and is an attraction in itself. That is not to belittle the impressive collection of 20th-century art that hangs in the museum, particularly works by Ernst and Klee

⬥ The art in Bonn isn't just hidden away inside museums

and those of the Rheinish Expressionists. ⓐ Friedrich-Ebert-Allee 2 ⓣ 0228-776 260 ⓦ http://kunstmuseum.bonn.de ⓛ 09.00–19.00 Tues–Sun, closed Mon ⓝ U-Bahn: Heussallee; tram: 16, 63, 66; bus: 610 to Heussallee

Rheinisches Landesmuseum (Rhine Regional Museum)

Explore the Rhine region's history, art and culture from the Stone Age to the present day in this recently revamped exhibition divided into various sections, from trade and tools to influential local individuals and artists. ⓐ Colmantstr. 14–18 ⓣ 0228-20700 ⓦ www.rlmb.lvr.de ⓛ 10.00–18.00 Tues, Thur–Sun, 10.00–21.00 Wed, closed Mon ⓝ Tram: 61, 62

RETAIL THERAPY

Strolling around the shops in Bonn's car-free old town is an excellent way to spend the day and see some of the city's historic buildings, too. Many of the shops are concentrated around the squares at Münsterplatz and Marktplatz and spill over down Sternstrasse and Remigiusstrasse in between. There are some particularly good designer boutiques for men and women, but if you prefer a bargain why not try Germany's biggest flea market, held on the third Sunday of the month between April and October in the Rheinaue park.

Body Gear Don't let the name put you off: this chic boutique sells exclusive designer menswear to the discerning gentlemen of Bonn. ⓐ Sternstr. 54 (in Einkaufpassage) ⓣ 0228-694 444 ⓛ 10.00–19.00 Mon–Fri, 10.00–18.00 Sat, closed Sun

Gentile Shoes, bags and accessories that will make you stand out from the crowd. ⓐ Am Dreleck 11 ⓛ 10.00–19.00 Mon–Wed, 10.00–20.00 Thur & Fri, 10.00–16.00 Sat, closed Sun

Kaufhof Bonn's biggest department store stocks everything from artisan food in the basement to cosmetics, clothing, jewellery and kitchenware. ⓐ Münsterpl. ⓣ 0228-5160 ⓦ www.kaufhof.de ⓛ 09.30–20.00 Mon–Fri, 09.30–16.00 Sat, closed Sun

Room Nine A bit pricey, but the unusual mix of interesting clothes, shoes and accessories includes many one-off items. ⓐ Sterntorbrücke 9 ⓛ 10.00–20.00 Mon–Fri, 10.00–18.00 Sat, closed Sun

Senfgarten Tucked away in a side street, this small shop stocks over 140 different types of mustard, as well as marmalades and oils. Many of the products are available for tasting. ⓐ Acherstr. 12 ⓣ 0228-390 7536 ⓛ 10.00–18.00 Mon–Sat, closed Sun

TAKING A BREAK

As in Cologne, café culture is alive and well in Bonn, particularly during summer, so there's plenty of choice.

Am Alten Zoll £ This incredibly popular beer garden has great views of the Rhine and shady trees for warm summer days. Cheap pizza and beer are the attractions. ⓐ Am Brassertufer ⓛ 11.00–23.00

Café im Kunstmuseum £ At the end of a visit to this modern art gallery, head to its café, with art on the walls, Italian coffee and

delicious cakes. ⓐ Friedrich-Ebert-Allee 2 ❶ 0228-230 059
ⓦ www.cafekumu.de 🕒 10.00–19.00 Tues–Sun, closed Mon

Pendel £ A great place to relax while shopping, this café-bistro serves
toasties, light lunches, coffee and cocktails. ⓐ Vivatsgasse 2a
❶ 0228-976 6064 🕒 10.00–01.00

Bon(n) Gout £–££ Trendy two-storey cafe with a wide-range of cakes
and coffee, plus snacks and full meals. ⓐ Remigiuspl. 2 (at the flower
market) ❶ 0228-658 988 🕒 09.00–01.00 Mon–Sat, 10.00–24.00 Sun

Miebach £–££ Sit out on this café's marketplace terrace with drinks,
cake or breakfast (served until 15.00). ⓐ Markt 8 ❶ 0228-692 500
🕒 08.00–24.00

AFTER DARK

Bonn is lively at night and stays open late, which suits the city's
students and tourists well. Even if you don't venture beyond the
centre, there are many restaurants to choose from and if you're
looking for culture then you're in luck, too: theatres, cinemas and
open-air music cater to every taste. Theatre and music listings in
English can be found in *Rhine Magazine*, available in bookshops.

RESTAURANTS

Brauhaus Bönnsch £ In addition to serving its own home-brewed beer,
this pub is a great place for traditional German fare that's heavy on
the meat. ⓐ Sterntorbrücke 4 ❶ 0228-650 610 ⓦ www.boennsch.de
🕒 11.00–01.00 Mon–Thur, 11.00–03.00 Fri & Sat, 11.00–24.00 Sun

San Telmo £ Good Spanish restaurant with wooden tables, great atmosphere and friendly service in Bonn's old town, not far from the centre. **ⓐ** Breite Str. 55 **ⓣ** 0228-638 663 **ⓛ** 18.00–23.00

Pirandello ££ Upmarket Italian restaurant in the town centre with excellent food and a large antipasti buffet. **ⓐ** Brüdergasse 22 **ⓣ** 0228-656 606 **ⓛ** 12.00–15.00, 18.00–24.00

BARS & CLUBS

Blow-up After midnight, it can be hard to move in this small bar, set in a former brothel. Old couches, mirrors, red lights and little-known grooves from the 1960s and 1970s make it a relaxed place to hang out. **ⓐ** Rathausgasse 10 **ⓣ** 0228-659 750 **ⓛ** 22.00–late

Casa del Gatto Cosy cellar bar that's popular for its cheap beer and food and its sunny terrace in summer. **ⓐ** Kaiserpl. 20 **ⓣ** 0228-995 522 **ⓛ** 11.00–02.00 Sun–Thur, 11.00–04.00 Fri & Sat

James Joyce Irish Pub Located in a 300-year-old building with low-beamed ceilings, the pub is hard to beat. Big screen and pool tables as well as hundreds of books and cosy corners make it the perfect choice for a rainy day. **ⓐ** Mauspfad 6–10 **ⓣ** 0228-369 5671 **ⓦ** www.jamesjoyce-bonn.de **ⓛ** 16.00–01.00 Sun–Thur, 12.00–03.00 Fri & Sat

Sovjetlokal Gum Bonn's only Russian pub, with the city centre's best range of vodkas, as well as cocktails and authentic snacks. **ⓐ** Sterntorbrücke 7 **ⓣ** 0228-631 312 **ⓦ** www.gum-bonn.de **ⓛ** 19.00–03.00 Mon–Thur, 19.00–05.00 Fri & Sat

ENTERTAINMENT

Beethovenfest Bonn Held usually from late August to late September, this internationally renowned festival doesn't just showcase Beethoven, but also focuses on contemporary composers. ❶ Information 0228-201 0345, Tickets 0180 500 1812 Ⓦ www.beethovenfest.de

Kammerspiele Bonn Stages a range of traditional theatre, music and dance productions. ⓐ Am Michaelshof 9 ❶ 0228-778 008

Poppelsdorf Palace In July and August this magnificent building becomes a backdrop for classical concerts. ⓐ Meckenheimer Allee 171 ❶ 0228-732 761, Tickets from Konzert & Theaterkasse in the Kaufhof department store ❶ 0228-697 980

ACCOMMODATION

Many hotels in Bonn also get booked out when trade fairs are being held in Cologne, and prices tend to be higher during these times.

Hotel Aigner £ Located in a quiet side street in Bonn's old town, this small family-run hotel is close to the area's restaurant and bars. ⓐ Dorotheenstr. 12 ❶ 0228-604 060 Ⓦ www.hotel-aigner.de

Hotel Ibis £ Basic, reliable rooms at reasonable rates, just north of the city centre. ⓐ Vorgebirgstr. 33 ❶ 0228-72660 Ⓦ www.ibishotel.com

Günnewig Hotel Bristol ££ This comfortable hotel, with rooms furnished in dark wood, is conveniently located between Poppelsdorf Palace and the university. ⓐ Prinz-Albert-Str. 2 ❶ 0228-26980 Ⓦ www.guennewig.de

Brühl & Phantasialand

Brühl is an attractive town, only 20 km (12 miles) south-west of
Cologne, popular with commuters because of its good shops and
restaurants, without the hectic pace of city life. It makes it onto
the tourist trail because it is home to the incredible Augustusburg
palace and Falkenlust hunting lodge, which were designated world
heritage sites more than 20 years ago by UNESCO, but the town has
other attractions worth seeing that many of the coach parties miss.
Another draw to the area is one of Europe's biggest theme parks,
Phantasialand.

GETTING THERE

By rail

A train from the Cologne's main railway station takes 15 minutes to
Brühl, less if you are getting on at Köln-West (Venloer Str.) or Köln
Süd (Luxemburger Str.) stations. The southbound tram on line 18 is
slightly cheaper and takes 30 minutes (for a one-way trip to Brühl,

BRÜHL OLD TOWN

Spare some time on your trip to enjoy Brühl's picturesque
old town, which is closed to cars and full of busy street cafés
and entertainers. Keep an eye out for the *Rathaus* (town hall),
which is located in a former Franciscan monastery established
in the 15th century. A number of half-timbered buildings and
pretty churches give Brühl a more rustic and old-fashioned
feel than either of its larger neighbouring cities.

you will need a City Plus 2b ticket). The best tram stop for the Augustusburg palace is Brühl-Mitte.

By road
It's no more than a 30-minute drive from Cologne on the A553 autobahn into Brühl.

SIGHTS & ATTRACTIONS

Phantasialand
Escape from reality for the day when you walk through the gates of Phantasialand, Germany's biggest and best theme park, just a few

🔴 *Thrills and spills in Germany's biggest theme park*

miles southwest of Brühl. Built on the Disney model, the huge park is split into themed areas that take the form of a street in old Berlin, a scene from the Wild West and Chinatown, to name just a few. The all-important rides are spread across the whole site and range from the child-friendly in Kinderland to the distinctly unfriendly Mystery Castle, with a spooky laboratory and scary 65 m (215 ft) drop.

Water rides are popular on hot, sunny days and the big round rafts of River Quest spin through tunnels and through white-water rapids, while the aptly named Wildwash Creek sends the brave around in a hollowed-out log at breakneck speed over various drops, so everyone gets a thorough soaking. Colorado Adventure is drier, but has you racing through tunnels and round sharp bends in a runaway train. The IMAX cinema technology used in Galaxy allows you to fly through space and survive meteor showers without moving (much).

It might be best to save a meal in one of the themed restaurants until after you've finished the rides. Perhaps one of the cinema or live shows would suit those who have just eaten.

If your children are less than 1m (39in) tall, they get in free, as does anyone visiting on their birthday (proof of date of birth required). ① 02232-36200 ⓦ www.phantasialand.de ⓛ 09.00–18.00, late Mar–early Nov; extended hours summer, special events Dec ⓝ U-Bahn 18 to Brühl-Mitte then bus 705. Admission charge

Schloss Augustusburg & Jagdschloss Falkenlust (Augustusburg Palace & Falkenlust hunting lodge)

Brühl's 'must see' sight, the Augustusburg Palace is a beautiful baroque building set in exceptionally well-maintained gardens, which remain in their original 18th-century French parterre design around vast lakes. Construction of the palace began in 1725 for the Archbishop of Cologne, Clemens August, but wasn't completed until

⬤ *The staircase is a masterpiece of Rococo overstatement*

1769, eight years after his death. Among the gems inside the palace are 18th-century frescoes and the magnificent marble staircase dating from 1740.

The Falkenlust hunting lodge stands proud at the end of a straight avenue leading from the palace and was originally built by Clemens August as a place to practise his beloved falconry. Visitors should note that the palace closes for 90 minutes at lunchtime on weekdays.

ⓐ Schlossstr. 6 ① 02232-44000 Ⓦ www.schlossbruehl.de
Ⓛ 09.00–12.00, 13.30–16.00 Tues–Fri, 10.00–17.00 Sat & Sun,
closed Mon, Feb–Nov; closed Dec & Jan. Admission charge

CULTURE

Max Ernst Museum

Opened in 2005, this 19th-century building in a parkland setting,
just ten minutes' walk from the old town, provides the perfect
venue for Brühl to display the work of its most famous son. Max
Ernst was born on Schlossstrasse in 1891 and went on to become
famous throughout the world for his 20th-century Dadaist and
Surrealist art. Many of his paintings, along with the majority of his
graphic works and bronze sculptures, are now housed in this museum.
There is also a collection of Ernst's photography, which provides an
interesting perspective on his contemporary artists and friends.
ⓐ Comestr. 42 ① 01805-743 465 Ⓦ www.maxernstmuseum.de
Ⓛ 11.00–18.00 Tues–Sun, 11.00–21.00 first Thur of the month,
closed Mon. Admission charge

Museum für Alltagsgeschichte (Museum of Everyday Life)

This faithfully restored half-timbered house is home to a cleverly
displayed selection of artefacts that aren't normally found in museums,
such as tools, clothing and dishes. Surprisingly engaging.
ⓐ Kempishofstr. 15 ① 02232-42642 Ⓦ www.bruehler-
museumsinsel.de Ⓛ 15.00–17.00 Mon–Sat, 11.00–13.00,
15.00–17.00 Sun. Admission charge

TAKING A BREAK

Brauhaus Brühler Hof £ Traditional hearty local food and thirst-quenching beer that will keep you going through the day. ⓐ Uhlstr. 30 ⓣ 02232-410 132 ⓛ 10.00–01.00

Café Feuser £ Top-notch coffee, cakes and home cooking make this a great place for lunch or a snack. ⓐ Kölnstr. 42 ⓣ 02232-42809 ⓛ 07.30–18.30 Mon–Thur, 07.00–14.00 Sat, 13.30–17.30 Sun, closed Fri

Eis-Café Bella Italia £ Indulgent ice cream sundaes and decent Italian coffee, served outside in sunny weather. ⓐ Markt 18 ⓣ 02232-150 185 ⓛ 10.00–20.30

Hof-Café £ Sit in the marketplace and eat delicious waffles, breakfasts and home-baked cakes while you sip coffee. ⓐ Markt 24 ⓣ 02232-42976 ⓛ 08.00–19.00 Mon–Fri, 08.00–18.00 Sat, 09.00–18.00 Sun

AFTER DARK

RESTAURANTS
China Palast £ A good Chinese restaurant in a handy central location. ⓐ Markt 6 ⓣ 02232-49795 ⓛ 11.30–15.00, 17.30–23.00

La Locanda £ Enjoy delicious Tuscan meat and fish dishes in this simple, rustic place, which has a log fire in winter. ⓐ Bonnstr. 73 ⓣ 02232-42075 ⓛ 17.00–22.00 Wed–Sat, 11.30–15.00, 17.00–22.00 Sun, closed Mon & Tues

Don Pancho £–££ This Argentinian restaurant does great grilled steak and fish, and always seems to be busy. **ⓐ** Kölnstr. 55 **ⓣ** 02232-43835 **ⓛ** 11.30–14.30, 17.30–23.30 Mon–Fri, 17.30–23.30 Sat, closed Sun

Balthasar Speiserei ££ Classic German and French cuisine with flair, plus an extensive wine list. **ⓐ** Wallstr. 30 **ⓣ** 02232-993 367 **ⓛ** 09.30–23.00 Tues–Sat, 10.00–17.00 Sun, closed Mon

CINEMA

Zoom Kino Not your standard big screen, but a huge sheet stretched across the town hall on summer evenings. Films shown subtitled in original version. **ⓐ** Uhlstr. 3 **ⓦ** www.zoomkino.de **ⓛ** Screenings at 20.00

ACCOMMODATION

Hotel Bonprix £ Rooms furnished in the most basic way, but comfortable and convenient for Brühl as well as Cologne and Bonn. **ⓐ** Hamburgerstr. 18 **ⓣ** 02232-15030 **ⓦ** www.hotel-bonprix.de

Hotel Ling Bao ££ Part of the Phantasialand theme park, this luxury family hotel is a large replica Chinese building. **ⓐ** Berggeiststr. 31–41 **ⓣ** 02232-36666 **ⓦ** www.phantasialand.de

Ramada Hotel Brühl-Köln ££ Comfortable rooms to the west of town. **ⓐ** Römerstr. 1–7 **ⓣ** 02232-2040 **ⓦ** www.ramada.de

ⓞ *'The train now leaving' Köln Hauptbahnhof is a high speed ICE*

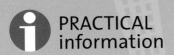

Directory

GETTING THERE

By air

Köln/Bonn Airport has become a hub for low-cost airlines flying from destinations all over Europe and within Germany. Reasonably priced flights from airports around the UK are easy to find and take between 1 hour 15 minutes and 1 hour 30 minutes. **EasyJet** (Ⓦ www.easyjet.com) flies from London Gatwick, East Midlands and Liverpool. **TUIfly** (Ⓦ www.tuifly.com) has flights from Manchester and Birmingham. **German Wings** (Ⓦ www.germanwings.com) flies from Birmingham, Dublin, Edinburgh, London Gatwick and London Stansted. Flights on **British Airways** (Ⓦ www.britishairways.com) and **Lufthansa** (Ⓦ www.lufthansa.com) leave from London Heathrow.

Scheduled flights from various cities in North America, South Africa and Australia fly into Düsseldorf and Frankfurt airports, which are 60 km (37 miles) and 180 km (112 miles) from Cologne respectively.

Many people are aware that air travel emits CO_2, which contributes to climate change. You may be interested in the possibility of lessening the environmental impact of your flight through Climate Care, which offsets your CO_2 by funding environmental projects around the world. Visit Ⓦ www.climatecare.org

By road

If you're coming from Britain and prefer the independence of driving your own car abroad, then Cologne, in the northwest of Germany, is a surprisingly short trip. Once you've made the hop across the English Channel by ferry or through the **Eurotunnel** (Ⓦ www.eurotunnel.com) to Calais, you should be able to cover the 400 km (250 miles) to Cologne in less than four hours. The E40 motorway will take you through France, into Belgium, past Brussels and Liège up to the Dutch border, when you should join the E314 motorway. This goes all the way to the German border, where it is best to turn onto the A4 autobahn and then the A1 for the last few miles into Cologne.

Alternatives to the Eurotunnel include **P&O Ferries** (Ⓦ www.poferries.com), and **SeaFrance** (Ⓦ www.seafrance.com), both of which sail from Dover to Calais.

◯ *Take the autobahn into the city*

Another possibility from the UK is coach travel. It's quite cheap to take the overnight coach from London Victoria, but so is a low-cost airline fare booked well in advance, and the coach journey takes a lot longer – between 11 hours 30 minutes and 13 hours; sometimes a change is required in Brussels. The coach arrives at Cologne's city centre bus station, behind the main railway station in Breslauer Platz. Eurolines buses can be booked through **National Express** in the UK (🆆 www.nationalexpress.com).

By rail

A practical alternative to air travel, particularly if you live in the south-east of England, is to catch the **Eurostar** (🆆 www.eurostar.com) to Brussels Midi and take a high-speed Thalys train to Cologne from there. The journey time from London Waterloo to Brussels is 2 hours 40 minutes and the second leg from Brussels to Cologne takes 2 hours 20 minutes. This combination of trains has the advantage that it brings you directly into the centre of Cologne, to the main railway station just next to the cathedral. Total journey time is approximately 6 1/2 hrs. The monthly Thomas Cook European Rail Timetable has up-to-date schedules for European international and national train services – 🆆 www.thomascookpublishing.com. For timetables and tickets, see also **Euro Railways** (🆆 www.eurorailways.com).

Of course, an entirely hassle-free way of arranging your holiday transport and accommodation is by booking a ready-made package break to Cologne with your travel agent. Booking your holiday in this way also gives you extra legal protection should unforeseen circumstances arise. If you choose to travel independently, it's worth paying the extra for travel insurance.

TRAVEL INSURANCE

However you book your city break, it is important to take out adequate personal travel insurance for the trip. For peace of mind, the policy should give cover for medical expenses, loss, theft, repatriation, personal liability and cancellation expenses. If you are travelling in your own vehicle you should also check that you are appropriately insured, make sure that you bring the relevant insurance documents and your driving licence with you.

ENTRY FORMALITIES

Citizens of the UK, Republic of Ireland and other EU countries, the USA, Canada, Australia and New Zealand are all permitted to enter Germany with a valid passport. A visa is only required if the duration of the stay is more than 90 days. Visitors from South Africa need to ensure that they have a valid passport and visa, return or onward travel tickets and sufficient funds for their stay.

Visitors to Germany from within the EU are entitled to bring their personal effects and goods for personal consumption and not for resale, which can be up to 800 cigarettes and ten litres of spirits. Those entering the country from outside the EU may bring 200 cigarettes (50 cigars, 250g tobacco), two litres of wine and one litre of spirits. No meat or milk products are permitted to be brought into the country from inside or outside the EU. For those flying in or out of Köln/Bonn Airport, customs can be contacted on
ⓣ 02203-955 7919

MONEY

Since 2002 the currency in Germany has been the euro, divided into 100 cents. Easily distinguishable notes are available in denominations of 5, 10, 20, 50 and 100 euros, while coins worth 1, 2, 5, 10, 20 and 50 cents, as well as 1 and 2 euros, are widely used. The Germans like to carry cash and in Cologne it's a good idea to do the same, because, as many tourists find out to their embarrassment, credit cards are not widely accepted.

Bureaux de change are few and far between in Cologne, so it is advisable to obtain your euros before you arrive, unless you're confident that German ATMs will accept your card. Two bureaux de change are located opposite the cathedral:

American Express ⓐ Burgmauer 14 ⓒ 09.00–18.00 Mon–Fri, 10.00–13.00 Sat, closed Sun

Travelex ⓐ Burgmauer 4 ⓒ 09.00–18.00 Mon–Fri, 09.00–14.00 Sat, closed Sun, Apr–Oct; 09.00–18.00 Mon–Fri, 10.00–13.00 Sat, Nov & Dec; 09.00–18.00 Mon–Fri, closed Sat & Sun, Jan & Feb

Look for the words 'International Geldautomat' on ATMs to show that they will take international credit and debit cards. There are few ATMs in the old town, but the shopping streets and the ring road have plenty of banks with 24-hour cash machines. Some German banks are affiliated to either MasterCard or Visa, so if your card does not work in one machine try one attached to a different bank.

Even some large shops and restaurants in Cologne will not take credit cards, so check the payment methods available before you order a meal or run up a bar bill. The Eurocard is the most commonly accepted card, but it is rarely issued by UK banks these days.

HEALTH, SAFETY & CRIME

Cologne's food and drinking water are safe for visitors to consume and should present no problems, except perhaps to vegetarians, who will find menus heavily meat-based.

Germany's healthcare system is excellent and thanks to a reciprocal agreement with the UK and most EU countries, their citizens are entitled to free or reduced-price medical and dental treatment on presentation of a valid European Health Insurance Card (EHIC). Apply for the EHIC on-line at www.dh.gov.uk/travellers and allow at least a week to receive the card.

If you need to be hospitalised in Germany there is a charge of €10 per day for a maximum of 14 days. Remember that the EHIC is no substitute for personal medical insurance and nationals of non-EU countries should also ensure that they have adequate medical cover before travelling.

Crime is not a big problem in Cologne, but keep an eye on your valuables in busy tourist areas, as pickpockets are always on the lookout for an easy target. The local police, with their slightly military-looking green uniform, are not a common sight in the tourist areas except during big events, when they are always present in large numbers. See Emergencies (pages 154–5) for more details.

OPENING HOURS

Germany deregulated store opening hours in 2007, so expect some later closing times than mentioned in this book. In general, most supermarkets are open from 08.00–20.00, Monday to Saturday. Other types of stores tend to open around 10.00 and close anywhere between 18.00 and 20.00. Many small shops are closed on Saturday afternoons. All of the city's shops are closed on Sundays, except for

bakeries, which open Sunday mornings, and kiosks. If you need anything from newspapers to beer outside regular hours, your best bet is one of the many kiosks or *Büdchen*, which open from the early hours until late at night and are also a popular source of cheap beer during festivals.

Banks open 08.00–12.00 and 14.00–16.00 Monday to Friday and are closed on Saturday. Post offices are open 08.00–12.00 and 14.00–18.00 Monday to Friday and 08.00–12.00 on Saturday.

All of the city's museums are closed on Mondays, but open on most public holidays (including public holidays that fall on a Monday) except Christmas and New Year's Day.

TOILETS

Public toilets in the city are few and far between, and you normally have to pay €0.50 to use them. There are good facilities in all the major museums and department stores.

CHILDREN

Kids are very welcome throughout Germany. Restaurants, cafés and even bars will generally be happy to cater for children and the preference for outdoor seating in summer removes any concerns about smoky air and fidgeting. The following sights and activities are guaranteed to keep youngsters entertained:

- **Climb the cathedral tower** Ideal for burning off some energy, the 509 steps to a great view of the city are safe and a big challenge to count. ● 09.00–16.00 Nov–Feb; until 17.00 Mar, Apr & Oct; until 18.00 May–Sept ● Bus/U-Bahn: Dom/Hbf. Admission charge

- **Chocolate Museum** (see pages 77–8) Fun, educational and delicious – a treat for children and adults alike.

- **Deutsches Sport & Olympia Museum** (see pages 76–7) Packed with sports memorabilia, interactive exhibits and information about the two German-hosted Olympic games.

- **City parks** (see pages 92, 112 and 114) Stadtgarten, Rheinpark and Volksgarten are all great green spaces for football, picnics and fun. Rheinpark has a miniature train to ride and Volksgarten has pedalos on the lake.

- **Kölner Zoo** (see pages 108–9) See animals from every continent, including elephants, bears, gorillas, insects and fish. Watch out for notices displaying feeding times to find out what the inhabitants like for lunch.

- **Cable car** (see page 111) Views are always more exciting when you are dangling from a wire high above a river.

- **Phantasialand** (see pages 135–6) One of Germany's largest theme parks is just 20 km (12 miles) from Cologne and filled with all kinds of rides from white-knuckle rollercoasters and flumes to more sedate carousels.

- **Ice cream parlours** These friendly Italian places can be found all over the city and their huge sundaes are a favourite with young and old, from morning until night.

COMMUNICATIONS
Internet
If email is your preferred method of keeping in touch then you'll find plenty of internet cafés around the city, including the following.

Giga-Byte ⓐ 7–11 Hohenzollering ⓣ 0221-652 6442 ⓛ 24 hours

Café Centro ⓐ Neumarkt subway station ⓛ 07.30–20.00 Mon–Fri, 08.00–16.00 Sat, closed Sun

---

⬤ *The bright yellow stamp machines are hard to miss*

Voice Store Köln HBF ⓐ Bahnhofsvorpl. 1 (in main railway station)
ⓣ 0221-139 7898 ⓛ 09.30–23.00

Phone

Most public phones in Cologne – look out for a pink and grey kiosk marked with a T – take coins, phone cards and credit cards and have instructions for their use in English; basically, lift the receiver, insert your payment method and dial the number. Phone cards can be purchased from post offices and many other shops.

Germany has a good mobile phone network, but before you travel, check with your service provider that you will be able to access the relevant network.

To phone home from Cologne, dial the international access code 00 followed by the relevant country code: UK 44, USA and Canada 1, Australia 61, New Zealand 64, Republic of Ireland 353, South Africa 27.

To call Cologne from abroad, dial your international access code and then the national code for Germany, 49, followed by the area code (221 for Cologne) and the number you require, which will be anything from four to nine digits long.

Post

The German postal service (Deutsche Post) is efficient and reliable. The bright yellow post offices and postboxes are easy to spot and it's best to buy stamps from a post office or an official machine outside. Stamps for postcards sent within Europe currently cost €0.65, or €1.00 for the rest of the world. There is a post office in the main railway station and at Auf de Ruhr 90, just off Breite Strasse.

ELECTRICITY

230 volts, 50Hz. European style two-pins plugs are standard and continental adaptors are suitable. Visitors with 110-volt appliances will need to use a voltage transformer.

TRAVELLERS WITH DISABILITIES

While the relatively modern buildings of most of Cologne's major museums provide good access for those with disabilities, much of the old town is full of steps and cobbles that will make getting around in a wheelchair difficult. Disabled access to the tram system is generally good, and while lifts down to U-Bahn stations are progressively being installed only those marked on the official maps are accessible. The city's taxis are mostly Mercedes and will not accommodate wheelchairs. The more modern hotels have the most appropriate facilities for disabled guests, but it's best to phone ahead and check that any specific requirements can be met.

Sources of UK advice for travellers with disabilities include:

Disabled Persons Transport Advisory Committee
Ⓦ www.dptac.gov.uk/door-to-door
Trip Scope ❶ 08457 585641 Ⓦ www.tripscope.org.uk

TOURIST INFORMATION

The English-speaking staff at the Cologne Tourist Board office in front of the cathedral towers are a useful source of maps, accommodation and event information.

Cologne Tourist Board
Old town ❷ Unter Fettenhennen 19 ❶ 0221-2213 0400 🕘 09.00–21.00 Mon–Sat, 10.00–18.00 Sun, Oct–June; 09.00–22.00 Mon–Sat, 10.00–18.00 Sun, July–Sept

Köln/Bonn Airport ⓐ Arrivals hall terminal 2 ⓛ 07.00–20.00
Mon–Fri, 08.00–20.00 Sat, 09.30–18.00 Sun

There are three official tourism websites that are crammed with
information in English about the city and its history, events and
facilities, as well as finding accommodation. They are:
Cologne Tourist Board ⓦ www.koeln.de/tourismus/koelntourismus/en
German National Tourist Board ⓦ www.germany-tourism.de
Cologne City Council ⓦ www.stadt-koeln.de/en

BACKGROUND READING

The Lost Honour of Katherina Blum by Heinrich Böll. Probably
his best-known novel outside Germany, this is a powerful and
prophetic account of the power of the tabloid press and the state.
One of Germany's foremost post-1945 writers, Böll was born and
lived in Cologne. He won the Nobel Prize for Literature in 1972 and
his novels and essays reflect his horrific experiences of war and
the typical, resilient *Rheinisch* humour that Cologne's population
is famous for. An archive of his work, in German only, is held at
Cologne Library on Antwerpener Strasse.

Emergencies

If the attendance of paramedics is necessary call the fire service number and request an ambulance (*Rettungswagen*).

Police ☎ 110

Fire service (and ambulance) ☎ 112

MEDICAL SERVICES

Lists of local doctors and dentists can be found in telephone directories, local newspapers or by contacting the relevant embassy. In an emergency your hotel should be able to summon a doctor. Lists of hospitals appear in local phone directories, too. In emergencies tourists with EHIC cards (see page 147) can receive treatment at any of these establishments at a charge of €10 per day for a maximum of 14 days. The following hospitals all have an outpatient emergency department (*Notaufnahme*).

Kliniken der Stadt Köln Krankenhaus Merheim ⓐ Ostmerheimer Str. 200 ☎ 0221-89070

Kliniken der Stadt Köln Krankenhaus Holweide ⓐ Neufelder Str. 32 ☎ 0221-89070

Krankenhaus der Augustinerinnen Köln ⓐ Jakobstr. 27–31 ☎ 0221-33080

Evangelisches Krankenhaus Köln-Weyertal ⓐ Weyertal 76 ☎ 0221-4790

POLICE

All of the city-centre police stations are open 24 hours a day and can be contacted on ☎ 0221-2290. In cases of theft you will have to report it to the police to obtain documentation for your insurance claim.

🔵 Maximinstr. 6, close to the main railway station and most convenient for the old town

🔵 Waidmarkt 1, near Severinstrasse U-Bahn station, to the south of the old town

🔵 Bismarckstr. 9, close to Stadtgarten, the park to the northwest of old town

🔵 Elsassstr. 27, not far from Volksgarten, the park south of old town

EMBASSIES & CONSULATES

Australian Embassy 🔵 Wallstr. 76-79, 10179 Berlin 📞 030 700 129 129
British Embassy 🔵 Yorckstr. 19, 40476 Düsseldorf 📞 0211-94480
Canadian Embassy 🔵 Benrather Str. 8, 40213 Düsseldorf 📞 0211-172 170
New Zealand Embassy 🔵 Friedrichstr. 60, 10117 Berlin 📞 030-206 210
South African Embassy 🔵 Tiergartenstr. 18, 10785 Berlin 📞 030-220 730
United States Embassy 🔵 Willi-Becker-Allee 10, 40227 Düsseldorf
📞 0211-788 8927

EMERGENCY PHRASES

Help!	**Fire!**	**Stop!**
Hilfe!	Feuer!	Halt!
Heelfe!	*Foy-er!*	*Halt!*

Call an ambulance/a doctor/the police/the fire service!
Rufen Sie bitte einen Krankenwagen/einen Arzt/die Polizei/
die Feuerwehr!
Roofen zee bitter inen krankenvaagen/inen artst/dee politsye/
dee foyervair!

INDEX

WHAT'S IN YOUR GUIDEBOOK?

Independent authors Impartial up-to-date information from our travel experts who meticulously source local knowledge.

Experience Thomas Cook's 165 years in the travel industry and guidebook publishing enriches every word with expertise you can trust.

Travel know-how Contributions by thousands of staff around the globe, each one living and breathing travel.

Editors Travel-publishing professionals, pulling everything together to craft a perfect blend of words, pictures, maps and design.

You, the traveller We deliver a practical, no-nonsense approach to information, geared to how you really use it.

Editorial/project management: Lisa Plumridge
Copy editors: Ismay Atkins & Lesley McCave
Layout/DTP: Alison Rayner
Proofreader: Wendy Janes

continued on page 160

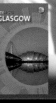

ACKNOWLEDGEMENTS & FEEDBACK

The publishers would like to thank the following individuals and organisations for supplying their copyright photographs for this book: Kermarrec Aurelien/istockphoto.com, page 60; Timothy Ball ©istockphoto.com, page 119; Martin Boose, page 7; Grant Bourne: pages 21, 25, 27, 37 & 101; Luke Daniek ©istockphoto.com, page 1; Inge Decker/Stadt Köln, page 95; Diedrich Dettmann/CSD Cologne, page 9; Anton Dimitrov ©istockphoto.com, page 40-1; DB AG/Louis: page 141; FC Köln, page 113; Globetrotter, page 84; Grischa Georgiew, page 13; Kate Hairsine, pages 120-1 & 128; Hans Klamm ©istockphoto.com, page 5; Köln Lichter, page 44; Kölner Seilbahn, 110; Kölner Verkehrs-Betriebe page 54; Leonard Lutz, page 19; Heinz Mülow/Stadt Köln, page 80; Phantasialand: page 135; Schokoladenmuseum Köln, pages 47 & 79; Sport Museum Köln, page 76; Stadt Brühl, page 137; Vladimir Stojkovic, page 57; Günther Ventur/Stadt Köln, pages 17 & 109; Jo Whittingham: pages 14, 39, 43, 65, 71, 83, 86, 93 & 150

Send your thoughts to
books@thomascook.com

- Found a great bar, club, shop or must-see sight that we don't feature?
- Like to tip us off about any information that needs a little updating?
- Want to tell us what you love about this handy little guidebook and more importantly how we can make it even handier?

Then here's your chance to tell all! Send us ideas, discoveries and recommendations today and then look out for your valuable input in the next edition of this title.

Email the above address (stating the title) or write to:
CitySpots Project Editor, Thomas Cook Publishing, PO Box 227, Coningsby Road, Peterborough PE3 8SB, UK.